'A brilliant collection of essays from autistic writers giving us personal insights into thoughts on relationship preferences and also valuable guidance for autistic people and those who love them. Demonstrating that autistic people often want to share their lives with others in a wide variety of set-ups, this book finally puts to bed the age-old myth of autistic people as isolated loners. The wonderful diversity of the autism population when it comes to choosing how to live, and who with, shines through.'

– Sarah Hendrickx, autistic adult, Autism Specialist and author

'*Love, Partnership, or Singleton on the Autism Spectrum* highlights the various joys, intricacies and challenges experienced by many on the spectrum in relationships. Featuring the experiences and views of those in relationships, some seeking partnership and individuals who choose to remain single, it asserts the right of autistic people to define our own contentment. Uplifting, thought-provoking and in places challenging, this book will undoubtedly lead to a general re-evaluation of long-held perceptions of relationships and what makes them work.'

– Dean Beadle, international autistic speaker and lecturer

'The desire to achieve a lasting and mutually fulfilling relationship can be very strong in someone with an Autism Spectrum Disorder. However, there may be significant challenges in finding a partner and maintaining the relationship. While we have considerable literature on the perspective of the partner who does not have an ASD, we have remarkably little on the perspective, experiences and achievements of the partner with an ASD. The wisdom and advice in this insightful book will be invaluable for both partners and contribute greatly towards an understanding of relationships from the ASD perspective.'

– Tony Attwood, Minds and Hearts Clinic, Brisbane

Love, Partnership, or Singleton on the Autism Spectrum

Books in the same series

Bittersweet on the Autism Spectrum
Edited by Luke Beardon and Dean Worton
Insider Intelligence
ISBN 978 1 78592 207 7
eISBN 978 1 78450 485 4

Aspies on Mental Health: Speaking for Ourselves
Edited by Luke Beardon and Dean Worton
Insider Intelligence
ISBN 978 1 84905 152 1
eISBN 978 0 85700 287 7

Asperger Syndrome and Social Relationships
Adults Speak Out about Asperger Syndrome
Edited by Genevieve Edmonds and Luke Beardon
ISBN 978 1 84310 647 0
eISBN 978 1 84642 777 0

Love, Partnership, or Singleton on the Autism Spectrum

Edited by Luke Beardon, PhD
and Dean Worton

Jessica Kingsley *Publishers*
London and Philadelphia

First published in 2017
by Jessica Kingsley Publishers
73 Collier Street
London N1 9BE, UK
and
400 Market Street, Suite 400
Philadelphia, PA 19106, USA

www.jkp.com

Library of Congress Cataloging in Publication Data
Names: Beardon, Luke, editor. | Worton, Dean, editor.
Title: Love, Partnership, or Singleton on the Autism
Spectrum / edited by Luke Beardon and Dean Worton.
Description: London ; Philadelphia : Jessica Kingsley Publishers, 2017. |
Includes bibliographical references.
Identifiers: LCCN 2016031988 | ISBN 9781785922060 (alk. paper)
Subjects: LCSH: Autistic people. | Autistic people--Sexual behavior. |
Interpersonal relations. | Man-woman
relationships. | Intimacy (Psychology)
Classification: LCC RC553.A88 R45 2017 | DDC 616.85/882--
dc23 LC record available at https://lccn.loc.gov/2016031988

British Library Cataloguing in Publication Data
A CIP catalogue record for this book is available from the British Library

ISBN 978 1 78592 206 0
eISBN 978 1 78450 484 7

Printed and bound in Great Britain

*To all those autistic individuals who have inspired
me and taught me so much; and my family – as
always, without you, I am nothing.*
Luke Beardon

*I would like to dedicate this book to all my family and
friends, and all those who have been there for me in
my life, and to Genevieve Edmonds who inspired these
books to be written, and will never be forgotten.*
Dean Worton

CONTENTS

PREFACE

Luke Beardon

I have been fortunate in my life to have met so many people on the autism spectrum, and even more fortunate that so many of those individuals have shared aspects of their lives with me. Each person with autism will have their own perspective on relationships and the meaning that they have, and this is reflected in the varying chapters in this book. At times throughout history autism has been viewed in many different ways, and to this day there is much debate around all sorts of areas relating to autism. Relationships have been written about from a professional perspective, and there is an abundance of autism theory that interested parties can read about. There is also a plethora of publications of autobiographical work which provides a rich insight into the perspectives of individuals.

This book aims to give a platform for people with autism to share their perspectives on what relationships mean to them. Each chapter brings its own style and its own story, with no one opinion or experience any greater or lesser in importance than another.

This book is not meant as a guide (though some may find aspects useful in their lives) nor is it in any way a definitive tome on the perspectives of all people with autism on relationships. What it is, though, is a fascinating collection of writing from a number of people who have taken the time and effort to identify what their thoughts and perspectives are around the notion of relationships.

Reflected in this book – and a familiar theme running throughout the 'Adults Speak Out' series – is the huge diversity to be found within the autism spectrum. It is so crystal clear on reading individual accounts that there can be no 'one size fits all' approach when it comes to relationships. I am sometimes asked 'Is it better for a person with autism to be in a relationship with another person with autism, or a non-autistic person?'; the answer here lies in the word 'matched'. If two individuals are well matched, then they are well matched – it simply does not matter whether they share a diagnosis or identity. Of course, some autistic people find that others with autism have a better intuitive understanding within a partnership, while some may find that a non-autistic person brings other advantages to the relationship.

I would imagine that most people much of the time find that there are bewildering complexities in relationships; however, I do think that when one or both partners are on the autism spectrum additional complexities can arise. Whenever I have had the opportunity to discuss relationships with people on the spectrum the most common theme that causes problems is a lack of understanding. It might be incredibly difficult (if not impossible) for a partner to understand certain aspects of life; this may go both ways – an autistic partner may find it difficult to understand a non-autistic partner, and vice versa. The solution to this issue seems to be acceptance; while one may not have a full understanding of a particular issue, if one fully accepts it it may go a long way towards it no longer being problematic.

When I first started working in the autism field the literature was very much on representing people with autism as loners, people who shunned contact with others and disliked people in general. Much has changed in terms of preconceptions since those days, and I believe that perception today is vastly different. Certainly it is the case that it is now recognised that people with autism can have highly successful relationships – be they friendships and/or intimate relationships. Sometimes those relationships may appear unconventional to the general population, but that does not diminish them in any way. I know of more than one very loving couple, for example, who live next door to one another – it may seem unconventional, but they often get comments from other couples along the lines of 'I wish we could do that, it sounds perfect!'; perhaps this is one of those examples where doing things just a bit differently can be extremely positive and rewarding. On that note, the authors who identify being celibate out of choice is notable. Very often it seems that individuals are judged on notions that the non-autistic deem important – and being with a partner might be an area that is seen as a criterion for 'success'. Some individuals with autism, however, may view this in the opposite manner – for them, success may well be a nice, comfortable, solitary existence free of anyone interrupting it!

One of the perennial stereotypes of the autistic individual is that of being socially 'aloof' – or, a loner. I have never subscribed to this – my understanding is that within the spectrum there is a parallel spectrum of 'sociability' – in other words, some individuals will prefer their own company and strive to avoid social situations, while at the other end some might crave company, parties, wide friendship groups and the like. This does not appear to be gender specific either; some women are quiet, perhaps shy – and may make for the perfect partner as a direct result. Some women may be more extrovert – and the same goes with the men on the spectrum.

One of the advantages of having a partner on the spectrum is the different perspectives that individual is likely to bring to the relationship. Having an 'alternative' view can be incredibly refreshing. I know several individuals who are the 'go to' person for possible solutions to problems that have arisen (including within relationships), and those solutions often make absolute sense. Having the ability to problem solve in an objective manner may not be a skill that all autistic individuals possess but it is certainly prevalent enough to warrant noting. Other qualities that are often found within the autism population (though, of course, not exclusively) include a quirky sense of humour (which can be invaluable in relationships), absolute honesty, determination to put others' feelings before their own, a driving need to strive for 'what is right' for their family and friends, and endless dedication to the relationship. I am not suggesting that these are more commonly found in the autism population, but they are certainly aspects that traditionally are not highlighted, so are worthy of note.

From a personal perspective, I know enough individuals with autism with whom I have a close relationship to be able to note that the loyalty and depth of feeling one can have is extraordinary. I know so many people who would do almost anything for a friend or partner, even if it is very much to their own detriment. The level of selflessness and altruism that can be found in the autism population is beyond doubt, irrespective of the perennial myth of individuals erring towards the self-centred.

My ongoing thanks to all contributors to this book, to Dean, and, as always, to my family.

Chapter 1

Different Loves for Different Folks

Wenn Lawson

Introduction by Luke Beardon

As is always the case Wenn has provided some excellent writing in this first chapter. In as an objective way as can be achieved Wenn has given some really useful guidance regarding all the various types of relationships that can be encountered. Wenn has long been an internationally acclaimed figure in the world of autism, and it is a huge honour to be able to include his writing within this book. Wenn has an ability to see things from a wide perspective, not just his, which is refreshing and useful to the reader. He also has a wide-ranging experience, and has learned about life and relationships from his own experiences as well as those many individuals he has met along the way. This first chapter is an excellent introduction into the world of autism and relationships.

Introduction

Intimate and romantic relationships are different to social relationships because they tend to be fewer in number, apply to only a few of our social contacts and are usually of a deeper and more personal nature.

According to Wikipedia the following defines intimate and romantic relationships: 'an *intimate relationship* is an interpersonal relationship with a great deal of physical and/or emotional intimacy. It is usually characterized by romantic or passionate love and attachment. Sexuality may or may not be involved...'[1]

Passionate or intimate?

Passionate is a word we use to describe having or feeling strong emotion about something or someone. For example, one can feel strongly about the issues surrounding global warming and the environment, but one could also describe being passionate about watching the football! On the other hand, a passionate relationship tends to imply one that is characterised by attachment, almost obsessive in nature and is deeply emotive. Romantic relationships may be passionate, but can also include the understanding that an intimate relationship exists between two people that is exclusive to them, with or without passion.

Are all social relationships intimate?

Social relationships tend to exist amongst groups of individuals (e.g. families, friends, clubs, societies) whereas intimate and romantic relationships are usually between two people at any one time. In some societies polygamy exists and a person may have more than one partner, but, they still tend to be 'with' only one of their partners at any one time. There are also some situations where being part of a couple involves a third person, so the couple become a 'threesome'. So, although a social relationship can be romantic, usually once it does so it changes the nature and tone of that relationship. This means we tend to think

---

1   Wikipedia (2016) 'Intimate relationship'. Available at http://en.wikipedia.org/wiki/Intimate_relationship, accessed on 2 August 2016.

of social relationships as broader, less intimate, based on different criteria and not limited or exclusive to a couple of individuals, but more inclusive of the broader community.

Intimate settings

Sometimes we talk about a 'setting' or place as one that has an intimate atmosphere. This usually means that the environment of that place or setting is conducive to creating a sense of quietness, calm, connection and wellbeing. It might be a restaurant lit by candle light and with soft music playing or it might be a room with dim lighting, a cosy couch and just the two of you at home. These are examples; there are several other situations that could also be described as 'intimate' (e.g. where an individual shares personally and deeply with another; where intimate knowledge is shared between a couple of individuals or a small group; where special times are shared with another or with family, such as the birth of a baby).

The term compassionate has several properties that might include the emotions of being passionate or it might not. Having compassion and being compassionate also involves strong feeling, but it might not be of an intimate nature so much as it might be more objective. For example, one might become aware of another's predicament and feel compassion for them without ever having met them (e.g. a people bound by poverty or disease).

If you are interested in understanding or exploring intimate or romantic relationships, this chapter might be useful to you.

Intimacy

Being intimate with another human being can be one of the most rewarding experiences one can have. But how does one go about finding this kind of relationship and maintaining it? Do all intimate relationships have to be romantic?

Is one intimate relationship enough or should we have lots of them?

To offer a suggestion for the first question, there are many kinds of intimate relationships and just as many ways to maintain them. Below are some types of intimate relationships you might experience, but not all are romantic:

Partner and partner (e.g. husband, wife, same sex couples)

Best friend and confidante to each other

Lover and lover

Psychologist and client

Psychiatrist and patient

Doctor and patient

Priest, pastor, rabbi or religious confidante

Parent and child

Social worker and service user and so on...

As you can see from the list above, some of these relationships are intimate and romantic, but others are not. To class a relationship as 'intimate' would require the sharing of personal information, trust, time, honesty, commitment and even private issues that you wouldn't just share with anyone, but someone who you would need to feel safe with and/or have a reason to share intimate information with.

There are even times of genuine intimacy that occur due to circumstances beyond our control. We might meet someone who 'is in the same boat' as us (in the same situation). This means that they are experiencing similar circumstances to us and it is the situation that triggers the intimacy. For example, when I gave birth to my second-born child I was in a cubicle where a new mum had just birthed a baby, but the baby died. The curtains were around her bed as the whole family shared in her grief. Once the family had left and the curtains were open again I offered my condolences. This new mum had managed to 'stay in control' whilst her family were present but, my words triggered her tears and she allowed me to comfort her. Although this intimate time was very real, after she left the ward I didn't see her again.

Intimate relationships can be long-lasting or they might be more fleeting. We all need intimacy in our lives. It enables us to share who we are with another human being and this nourishes our soul and can help to rejuvenate our spirit.

Some intimate relationships exist because of the intimate nature of what is shared. For example, doctor with patient, counsellor with counsellee or solicitor with client. At times it is really important to make sure the professional we are sharing personal information with is trustworthy and has our best interests at heart.

So it might not be difficult to get an appointment to talk to a psychologist, for example, and set up some time to share the concerns you have about your life. But finding the right psychologist who is tuned in to your particular needs might not be so easy. If you think you need to see a psychologist, a relationships counsellor or someone similar it's a good idea to write them a letter outlining who you are, any diagnosis you might have and the expectations you have for any potential relationship. At least, this way, you can vet their responses and assess the potential for a positive outcome. Should we do this with all other potential intimate relationships? Maybe we should! It's usually not a bad idea to put things in writing and try to clarify intentions, expectations and considerations.

Friendship

You might not be interested in seeing a counsellor, but you might be interested in developing a safe intimate relationship with another person of similar interests to yourself. Finding a 'friend' and soulmate to share everyday personal things with is very special. Such a friend might be someone already within your family or social group. They might exist on an e-mail list or cyber support group. I have friends whom I consider to be close intimate friends who I share personally with, but whom I either haven't met 'in the flesh' yet, or have only met a couple of times. I have found the internet to be a useful place for finding and building personal friendships. Of course one must be careful when using the internet because some individuals might not be who they say they are. Finding a reputable site and checking this out thoroughly is very important.

There are some rules about internet relationships. It is never OK to give someone your personal banking details or any information about your financial situation. As you get to know someone and meet them in real time, you will get to know what to share and what is to remain private. A good rule is never share personal information that you don't feel comfortable with. How can we tell what is comfortable; what is OK? I know this can be difficult. Below are some guidelines that might help.

Public

Intimacy and being intimate with another person is usually not for the public arena. Relationships that are non-intimate have a number of characteristics that define them as being different to intimate and/or romantic relationships. Much of the understanding and the social skills needed for non-intimate relationships are covered elsewhere. You can also read more in *Sex, Sexuality and the Autism Spectrum* and *Friendships, the Aspie Way*.[2] These two books are a couple of many that now exist to give pointers for understanding and building successful relationships.

---

2   Lawson, W. (2005) *Sex, Sexuality and the Autism Spectrum*. London: Jessica Kingsley Publishers. Lawson, W. (2006) *Friendships the Aspie Way*. London: Jessica Kingsley Publishers.

However, to start with even those relationships that might develop into more intimate relationships can be quite public and non-intimate. It is very common to share in what is called 'small talk'. This entails any information concerning topics such as 'the weather'; the prices of groceries or shop products and how they might have changed; the price of petrol or gas; passing comments about the environment, the sports results or the property market. These are things that might be considered as 'of interest' to lots of people but without personal or private revelations. They are meant to be a part of fleeting conversations and, as such, are not meant to be gone into at any depth. If you are wondering what the point of 'small talk' is, I think it might be a familiar NT (neurotypical or non-autistic) way of sharing time with another person but without getting too involved. It's a bit like when someone smiles at you; they are simply saying 'hi' but without needing to go any further into conversation. Quite often a smile can help someone feel good about themselves and their day. A good rule where smiles are concerned is that we reply in kind; they smile, we smile back. It is often not necessary to speak or take it any further. If someone requires a verbal response from us, they usually request one by being verbal themselves. For example, a smile might be accompanied by words such as 'have a nice day' or 'can I help you' and so on.

Developing intimacy

If one's conversation moves beyond 'small talk' then one would say that the relationship might be developing and growing into something more. This still doesn't mean that it is becoming an intimate relationship, though, it just means things are becoming more friendly. Initially, 'small talk' can be a useful step in the right direction. Next, if one wants to develop a more intimate relationship one needs to increase the range of interests within the conversation. For many of us this can be difficult because we tend to have quite narrow and specific interests that might not be interesting to the person we want to develop a relationship with.

If the relationship is doctor and patient, of course, the doctor will only be interested in our medical needs. So, although we might share some very personal and intimate information with them, it is only for medical purposes, not for furthering any personal relationships. This might be slightly different when it comes to a therapy relationship with a counsellor. We might share personal information of a similar medical nature to that we might tell the doctor. But we also share on a personal level about our emotions, thoughts, problems and difficulties. So, although this might seem more intimate it is generally one sided. That is, we talk to the therapist about our problems as a means to exploring resolution to our difficulties, but the relationship is not the place for the therapist to air their problems. It is not a two-sided relationship where we both share our problems together.

Real intimacy can only grow as individuals share and relate together as equals, with both parties allowing the other to know their thoughts, fears, hopes and dreams and so on. It is very hard trying to listen to someone talk about things one isn't interested in. But if we want to foster intimacy then learning to listen to the other person and not always talking about things that interest us is paramount. Below is a recipe that might be useful for developing our listening skills.

Recipe for successful listening

- *Plan time* to listen. This means stopping your own activity and creating space for time with your friend. This could vary according to the level of importance, but usually it means allowing half an hour to an hour where your friend gets to share their perspective without being interrupted by other concerns.

- *Body language*: Part of actively listening means *acknowledging* what one hears. If we lean forward and look attentive, as well as responding in a positive manner to show we have heard and understood what has been said, then our friends will 'feel' listened to. This is very important because *feeling heard, understood and appreciated* is part of the recipe for successful intimate relationships.

- *Response*: Successful listening also requires *action*. If my friend has shared their concerns or opinions they might require me to 'act' upon what they have said by giving them some feedback. Even if we have a different viewpoint or don't agree with our friend, it's important to affirm them and not share our opinion at this time. If they ask for our opinion, then we might tactfully state it, but more as a 'by the way' rather than as a 'fact' statement of truth or a demand that they must see it 'our' way.

Romantic relationships

Romantic relationships are not always truly intimate. Sometimes romance can foster sexual attraction and sexual desire without our having to get to know the person first or reveal much about our own hopes and dreams. Of course, for most of us and our relationships, one hopes that intimacy will develop as the romance blossoms and as we get to know each other. Below are some points to consider as we seek to develop both an intimate and a romantic relationship. If it's a mate or life partner and companion we are looking for, read on!

Things to consider in looking for a mate

1. Did your relationship develop from friendship? Usually friendship tends to be a good foundation for intimate or/and romantic relationships.

2. Do you have similar interests? Although 'opposites attract', sharing in similar interests helps to maintain the relationship.

3. Do you share the same values? If you don't, you might have difficulty fostering harmony.

4. Is this person interested in you in the same way that you are interested in them? Remember, it needs to be two way!

5. Do your friends or family agree with your choice? If they don't it will be harder (although not impossible) to access the support your relationship might need.

6. Are there niggling doubts about this person's ability to commit to this relationship? Best not to 'put all your eggs into one basket' if that basket has holes in it.

7. Can you happily imagine waking up beside this person for the next 50 years? If this thought creates discomfort or panic inside you, this person is not the right one for you.

8. If there are some discomforts between you, is this person happy to talk them over and see a counsellor if you feel it would be helpful? If they are not it could get a bit lonely and difficult trying to work things out on your own all of the time.

9.   Do you both have the same goals for a relationship?

10. Is this person willing to take the time to get to
     know and share themselves with you? It's OK to go
     slowly, as long as the relationship is growing and not
     stagnant.

The above are just a few of the typical questions that need to
be asked as a romantic and intimate relationship develops
into a long-time partnership. Some individuals will want to
consider marriage or moving in together. Each of us has a life
before we met the other and this means that we will bring
our own 'baggage' into our relationships. It is this baggage
that can weigh each of us down, if it isn't sorted first.

Some myths about romantic and intimate relationships

'We love one another, this is all that matters.' Love
     doesn't pay the bills and what will happen if we don't
     'feel' loving one day?

'I know that this person will meet all of my needs.' No,
     they won't.

'This person will settle down after we are married.'
     Usually what you see is what you get. People change
     very little over time.

'Being married will change them.' This is unlikely. What
     is more likely is that pressure, responsibilities and
     commitments increase as you build a home together
     so, rather than settling down, they might find it even
     more difficult to cope and opt out even more than
     they did before.

'The wedding is the hardest issue, being married and
     together is the easy bit!' For most of us, even though

arranging a wedding is difficult, it is only one day of your life. Being married might last much longer, perhaps a lifetime.

'Having children will fulfil and complete us.' This is not the best reason to have children. Of course, children do fulfil and complete one, but children grow up and leave home. We each need to have a life of our own and not aim to live it through our children.

'We can sort out our roles, who does what and when, after we move in together.' Again, this is best sorted before you move in together.

Tips for successful intimate partnerships

- Take time to get to know one another and build a solid friendship first.

- Get to know, understand and appreciate each other's differing opinions, interests, approaches and learning styles (see Lawson 2005 for a fuller description of this topic).[3]

- Practise accepting and loving each other each day, even when it's difficult.

- Sometimes, love is not a feeling, it's an act of your will. This will mean choosing to forgive each other when things don't go your way.

- During the early stages of any romantic relationship it is common to perform for our partner and want to please them. For example, we might take extra care in our physical presentation, manners, general behaviour and demands. However, no one can keep

---

3   Lawson, W. (2005) *Sex, Sexuality and the Autism Spectrum*. London: Jessica Kingsley Publishers.

this up for very long and we soon move past this behaviour and settle into being more ourselves. If our partner doesn't like who we are, we might need to ask ourselves if they really are the right person for us before we commit to living together. Feeling 'comfy' with one another is vital to the success of this type of relationship. I've heard it expressed as 'when I'm with her/him, it's like coming home'. Or, 'we fit, like a well worn favourite pullover'.

- We also need to remind ourselves that no one person can meet all of our needs and we shouldn't expect them too. Each of us is a complicated individual so we need different relationships with different people for different reasons. This might be why guys like to meet up with other guys and girls have their girls' nights out!

All relationships go through ups and downs. This is normal and it can be a positive in developing character. Learning how to resolve conflict appropriately and move on in our relationships keeps our relationships healthy.

My Love (written for my wife)

It wasn't always this way. The joy of knowing you and sharing in your life has taught me that I am able to love and accept myself.

In your presence I come to life in a way that I have never experienced before. This rag doll who is losing his stuffing becomes the musical clown, so full of colour and vitality.

You set me free from the demands of self-introspection and its ugly forest of gloom.

In its place I am able to walk through sun lit woods and enjoy choruses of bird song.

Your smile delights my eyes and the peace in my
soul rolls over me like the gentle waves of a
calm ocean.

So soothing is your voice to my ears that even
the roar of my lions within cannot shatter
it. Thank you, my love, for your quiet
assurance and humble vulnerability.

To you I owe a never-ending debt, my life.[4]

Good communication

Good communication is another key to successfully
developing and maintaining intimate and romantic relationships. It certainly isn't easy to communicate with another
person at times. I think this is because all communication
has several aspects to it. The words one hears are just one
part of the communication and sometimes it's what is *not*
said that can create the difficulty. Consider the scenario
below:

'I'll wash the dishes,' to which you might reply 'OK'.
Later on during the evening your partner or friend
seems a bit distant and there is a discomfort between
you, but you don't know why. You say 'Are you OK,
is everything alright?' To which they reply, 'Well, I
cooked the meal, you might at least have offered to
wash up.'

So, you see, even though your friend might have said that
they would wash the dishes they actually wanted you to! It is
so hard to read what people really want. It might be a good
idea to give your partner permission to be 'blunt' with you.
Say it like it is. As autism spectrum individuals we tend to
be literal and single minded. Quite often this is an asset. We

---

4   First published in Lawson, W. (2006) *ASPoetry*. London: Jessica
Kingsley Publishers.

are loyal, truthful, trustworthy, committed and care deeply and passionately for those things we are interested in. This includes our relationships with others. However, our being single focused can mean we miss things that might be obvious to others. So having our partner or friend spell it out for us is helpful.

Setting the foundation for good communication

It's interesting that many of the things that cause conflict between people are based on how they perceive the other person's actions and words, rather than the actual circumstances they may be about. For example: 'You always act impulsively and never consider my feelings or our budget!' Such a communication could be a product of the owner feeling threatened or feeling like they are not in control. The person hearing the words might perceive them as an accusation and feel 'put down'. This could then cause that individual to defend their action and themselves. The need to defend oneself against another could be conceived of as an act of war! The communication could have gone differently, for example: 'Darling, can we talk about this decision? I'm feeling worried about our budget. Do you think we can afford this?' Such a communication does a couple of things. It says to your partner that you are interested in what they think, rather than putting them down. It also spells confidence in negotiations, rather than promoting the need for a fight.

We all need to feel valued, important, listened to and loved. When we take the time to listen, rather than react to our partners and they reciprocate, we each hear that we are more significant than the issue under debate. This message is far more important to building success in our relationships than any other.

Common communication behaviours in autism

Below are some common behaviours that many of us, as autism spectrum individuals, use to communicate what we think. At times NTs use these too, but they might be aware of what they are doing whilst we might not.

Common autism spectrum behaviours that might negatively impact upon communication

- *Not noticing or hearing when spoken to*: We can get so focused upon an interest that we might not hear what someone says to us. This could be interpreted as 'bad manners', 'being rude' or simply that we are not interested in our partner or friend. One way to help overcome their interpretation of our behaviour is to let them know this is how it is for us and to give them some pointers about how to join our interest. In this way we have a better chance at good communication. Sending e-mails, writing notes and finding ways to access our attention would be useful.

- *Needing to complete a ritual or routine*: Structure is very important to us. Having routines and specific ways to progress through the day can be vital to our being able to access 'time', activity and even thought. Again, this might be interpreted negatively by our friend or partner. Letting them know that we need structure, and even asking them for their input into our day, might be a good way to overcome their negativity and even help create a sense of their feeling useful and helpful.

- *Obsessive thinking*: Being stuck in our thoughts and thinking processes causes us to exclude everything else. This is not uncommon for us. The need to go over and over something in our minds is part of how we process a scenario and work out what it all means. Our partners, however, might consider this unnecessary and find it irritating. Explaining our needs to them might help them understand us better. Together we might even be able to 'brainstorm' the situation, bring it to a comfortable conclusion and put it to rest.

- *Being literal*: Quite often people use metaphors in their conversations to assist them in describing their emotions and responses. This can be problematic for us because we might interpret them literally. For example: 'here's mud in your eye' might cause us to feel threatened. But this metaphor means 'I wish you good luck.' Good communication can only happen when both parties perceive the conversation in the same way. So explain when you don't feel comfy with something being said and ask the person to 'say it plainly'. *Build Your Own Life* has a concise dictionary of metaphor at the back – worth exploring if you are interested.[5]

- *Overload*: This happens for us when we try to do, say or think too much at any one time. When I am writing or working at my computer I don't cope with being spoken to, demanded of or even having the radio on at the same time. This doesn't mean we are all like this, it's just an example. In fact, we are all more different than we are alike! But, the principle is the same. It might be different things overload us, but we tend to get overloaded more quickly than the NT population.

---

5   Lawson, W. (2003) *Build Your Own Life: A Self-Help Guide for Individuals with Asperger's Syndrome.* London: Jessica Kingsley Publishers.

*Some more ideas that might help
improve communication*

- Understanding each other's *learning style* and communication system is very important to good communication. For example: are you a visual person who needs to 'see' the picture before you can comprehend it? If so, words might only confuse you and not help. Putting things into a map of some sort or finding a way to illustrate the issue might be better. If words do it for you, though, writing it out might be the most helpful.

- If you are anything like me you might find it difficult to be organised. Making *lists* and using an *electronic organiser* might help. I forgot my partner's birthday once! Forgetting dates and appointments that are significant to our partners or friends could be interpreted by them as our not 'caring'. This isn't true, we simply forgot!

- Because I take a bit longer to *process information*, some conversations move too fast for me. Maybe this happens for you too. It's perfectly fine to ask a person to slow down their conversation and give you more time to process what is being said. You might be the person on the other side of this scenario and you might need to slow down yourself or give your partner or friend more processing time. Sometimes, a ten second rule is a very useful tool! (Giving someone ten seconds between hearing and responding).

- *Checking in* on what we hear or what we say to each other is very useful in good communication. This does not mean 'parroting back' what we hear but, rather, putting what we heard into our own words. If we got the understanding wrong, it gives the other person a chance to rephrase what they said and make sure we are each clear on the communication issued.

Some positives in autism spectrum communication styles

- *Single mindedness*: Because we are single minded and good at being focused we are usually good at following through with the things we say or do. If we have some timing issues, these need to be accommodated, worked out or understood, but we do not usually fail in our commitment. Our 'yea' is our 'yea' and our 'nay' is our 'nay', so to speak.

- *Routine*: Although we may not be good at spontaneity and surprise, structure and routine have some advantages. You always know what you will get, what comes next and what to expect. When my partner gives me her Christmas list, I can relax and not worry about whether or not I buy her the right gift!

- *Loyalty*: Being loyal and committed to our friends and partners is definitely a plus. It gives us the edge when it comes to hanging in there with someone and being determined to stick with them and see things through.

- *Kindness*: Kindness is a quality that can help support our relationship even when we might not understand our own or our partner's behaviour. Kindness can buy time and help us learn to look at the bigger picture.

- *Being able to relate to either gender*: Because we tend to 'fall for' the person and not their gender the chances of our finding and building an intimate relationship are higher than for those individuals who are exclusively heterosexual or homosexual. Of course, one might be exclusively drawn to one sex or the other, but it is interesting that so many of us, as autism spectrum individuals, don't let gender ID get in the way.

Some guidelines for relationship maintenance

- It's wise not to let the sun go down on your anger. This just means aiming to reach a place of conflict resolution, before bedtime. Even if you agree to disagree, this is better than going to bed together and lying beside one another with your heart pumping away because you are upset.

- Practise keeping an open mind and be available to listen to each other and touch base often.

- Don't allow the chores and responsibilities of everyday life to crowd out personal time together or necessary recouping on your own.

- Communicate together often. Don't take it for granted that your friend or partner can 'read' your mind. S/he cannot!

- Leave one another encouraging notes. It always makes me feel good when I find a 'love note' in my sandwich box or on my computer.

- I think walking around one's neighbourhood together and taking in the sights and sounds is a lovely thing to do together. But, however you enjoy your time together, make time for frequent outings or go on a date to your favourite restaurant, or something that suits you both.

- Although all autism spectrum individuals are different, we tend to share in some core characteristics. So educate yourself about the autism spectrum and learn to accept and understand yourself. If you have an intimate relationship with an NT individual you might need help to understand them, and them to understand you.

- Never criticise, expose or put your friend 'down' but always speak highly of them.

- Learning to celebrate who we each are and to welcome our differences can only be a good thing.

So, there you have it. This chapter is not the total story about building and maintaining intimate and romantic relationships, but it might be a good place to start.

Chapter 2

Knowing, Being, Living
I Am One

Tracy Turner

Introduction by Luke Beardon

Tracy has contributed an interesting chapter for a book on relationships – in that she explores what it means for her to not have one! Sometimes autism is associated with being unconventional; Tracy has proffered her insight into what may be deemed by many as an unconventional choice, that of very deliberately choosing to be single. Tracy mentions a few times that she is, perhaps, selfish in some way – but, having the pleasure of knowing her, I do not agree. She reasons well in her writing and demonstrates logic behind her perspective – while acknowledging that other views are perfectly valid. Choosing not to be in a relationship and choosing not to have children may not be 'the norm', but Tracy provides an interesting perspective as to why she has made those choices. One of the many interesting aspects of the chapter that stands out for me is how Tracy notes that she was a different person when in a relationship, and refers to the fact that when she became single she reverted to what might be regarded as her true self; she writes 'I am so much happier being true to myself.' Selfish? I don't think so. Sensible? Absolutely.

Being single for me is a matter of choice, not a place I have found myself in. It is a safe place, a place of sanctuary that feels right. I don't think I have ever been the sort of person that just does what is expected of them. I have always stood out as being a bit weird or different, and that is okay with me. It has not always been like that, of course, but it is the result of a life journeyed and a story that has unfolded.

As a child, particularly a teenager, I desperately wanted to fit in. I can remember many, many a night crying to my mum that I had no friends and nobody liked me. Usually you can pacify a child that this is not true but, unfortunately, it was. I just didn't seem to fit! I went to an all girls' school and I was not in the slightest bit interested in anything they had to say. All they could talk about was boys, jewellery, make up, pop stars (fairly normal stuff I guess), but I just did not get it. All I wanted to do was learn and read. I really had no other interests. I didn't do shopping or make up or hair or all those girly things that seem to bond girls together, at all, ever! Not great for the popularity stakes but I couldn't fake it either. That just isn't me. If nothing else, I can honestly say, I preferred (and still do) to stay true to who I am.

As an outsider looking in (and of course this is just my personal opinion), I do believe that a lot of people just do what is expected of them, without necessarily thinking about it or planning it. Lots of people get married or find a partner and have kids, it is the expected norm in our society. They maybe do not think beyond the cute, cuddly baby stage to the fact that the child will grow up. It just seems to be a natural progression for a lot of people. Sorry to those who disagree and I know you parents all love your kids. Some, I know, however, would say that no matter how much they love their kids, and they do; if they had their time over, and knew what they know now, they would choose more wisely. This is a perfectly understandable view in my book. Children take over your whole life (especially for the woman, who generally does the majority of the care). You have to put them first. Men on the other hand seem to carry on much as before, with the occasional child care duties thrown in (sorry to all the great house husbands and carers out there, this is just a generalisation). I apologise if this is not true for you; but among my friends and family and people I know, this just seems to be the way of things. I wonder, did these people consider this was an option when they made their cute, cuddly baby – maybe, maybe not. I think it is a decision requiring rather a lot more thought. I decided I did not want my life overtaken by a little, soon to be a big, person, and that is despite loving children very much. I am a primary school teacher and love working with kids, I also adore my nephew and niece and spend a lot of time with them, even holidaying with them and having them to stay. However, I know I can give them back, go home to my house, my peace and quiet, to read, write and walk my dog, and do what I do. I know having noise 24/7 would drive me to distraction, as well as constantly being 'at' you, wanting this and that and the other. Does that make me a bad person? I don't think so, maybe just a sensible one.

So what does that have to do with being single you may well ask yourself? Well, as a Christian, if I wanted kids I would have to be married and have a stable home to bring up a child (my rule, not just the Church's). I don't need to do this if I don't want a child. That has not always been my wish though. I wanted four children once, then reality took its grip and I realised I probably wouldn't be the best mother or partner. Maybe I'm too selfish, I don't know if being Aspie makes you selfish. They say it can show itself as being self-centred or egocentric, so maybe. I think I do have a lot of time and thought for others, However, on the realistic side, I think I'd be hell to live with, and I do like a lot of time to myself too.

I have my rules and routines you see. Like most Aspies everything has to be just so. It has to be done at the right time and in the right way – my way! I could compromise, but I am not prepared to, therefore it just makes it easier to be alone.

I can do what I want and as long as my dog is fed, loved and walked (three times a day usually) I don't need to answer to anyone else. That suits me just fine.

Do I get lonely? Well, yes, sometimes I suppose I do. Not so much for conversation (though sometimes I yearn for a chat after a day alone). I do miss the company. It would be nice to have someone to go out with or just sit quietly with. Someone to give you a hug now and then or offer some advice with difficult decisions regarding money, tax or insurance and things I don't understand too much. However, I'm guessing those wouldn't be a great reason for having a significant other, so I am probably best on my own.

It has not always been this way though. I did have a fairly 'odd' relationship with a guy in my 20s. I think it served a need for both of us at the time. I cannot say he was my type or I was in love with him or anything like that. We were mates basically. He'd just come out of a relationship and I was lonely and sad (my Mum had died) and I desperately needed to feel loved by someone, anyone. He just happened to be there. I think he probably used me; I think I let him! We did share similar interests and did enjoy each other's company. I think on reflection I wanted more than he was prepared to give me. Like many women, I was more emotionally invested than he was. I needed someone I could constantly rely upon, he couldn't (or wouldn't) give me that. He was probably very patient with me. I in turn pretended to be someone I am not. There is only so long that can go on. There was fault on both sides, though if I'm honest I blamed him for the failure of the 'relationship', if you can call it that. Looking back, I realise it would never have worked. Isn't hindsight such a wonderful thing? We kept in touch, although speak rarely these days. He said afterwards that I had changed. Actually I just went back to being the 'me' I was before I tried to be someone else; someone I thought he could like or love. I am so much happier being true to myself.

The older I get the more comfortable I am in my own skin. I am more honest with myself, and with others. I am quite happy to say 'no sorry I can't do..., go..., be in that place'. I make choices which are sensible for me and which means life is easier or more manageable for me. Again, I suppose that may sound selfish. However, I have no one else who will put 'me' first, so I need to make sure I do it, for myself. I make choices based on my health, my mental state and therefore my wellbeing. Other people looking in might say I miss out on all the fun. However, what is fun for them is invariably not 'fun' for me. I make no excuses anymore, I just say it like it is. I'm happy being me. Being autistic is hard enough in itself without trying to constantly pretend. People I can generally take or leave (with the exception of my family and a few good friends). Places and social events I can definitely happily leave (unless my presence is absolutely required – special birthdays, weddings, etc.), when I will make a special superhuman effort. Friends, I have a few, not too many, but enough. I have male friends, mates, buddies. They tend to be on a work kind of basis where I know the rules and what is expected. That's good enough for me.

Being single is not for everyone, but it suits me. Some people end up single through circumstance, divorce, bereavement; this could be sad or it could be liberating. I'm single by choice and just find it makes things less complicated (I mean flirting, what is that, I definitely can't do it and don't get it!). I can be my own boss, make my own decisions, spend my own money, choose my own holiday, wallpaper, what to watch on TV, what to do at the weekend...the list goes on. I'm quite stubborn and fiercely independent, so it is probably just as well. I think it would take a saint to put up with me. Being single gives me the freedom to be wholly myself and right now that is what is most important to me.

Chapter 3

Man in Progress

Alex Wilkinson

Introduction by Luke Beardon

This autobiographical narrative of a range of relationships interspersed with Alex's thoughts and feelings about those relationships makes for a fascinating read. His writing is insightful and a pleasure to read, and a wry sense of humour is rarely far away. Alex is very honest in his writing and provides a clear account of his experiences, and his perspective of them. It is difficult reading of some of the terrible times, for example at school – even more saddening is that his experiences are far from unique. Alex also demonstrates just what a gap there can be between emotions and emotional recognition – both in self and in others. Perhaps this is one of the most difficult aspects of autism for some people, the lack of understanding in terms of knowing what is being felt, and having to work out what other people are feeling. In most relationships the closer two people are the more they share their feelings. For some people with autism this must be hugely frustrating, when it would be especially useful for people to openly share what they are feeling from the outset! Unfortunately, this is rarely the case.

Imagine a middle-aged man who's just on the verge of decline: his posture is hunched from years spent sedentary in front of a TV/laptop; his belly a little rotund from countless calorific fast-food binges; his head balding; his self-esteem decimated on account of his life story; his eyes belie his inability to communicate effectively. Now completely forget what you've just read, because that's not me (at least, not yet).

Most self-help books make bold claims in the introduction, usually starting with modal verbs that imply a solution to the reader's questions, e.g. *After reading this book, you will be able to...*'. When I found out about this project I found myself keen to engage, yet at the same time uncertain how to do so. This is in part because I've read many self-help books without finding them useful. I don't want to come across as someone who claims to know something when in reality their knowledge and/or delivery of a topic is abjectly inept: I don't want to give a false impression. Further, I don't want anyone to make assumptions based upon my veracity as a writer or, more to the point, a human being. Consequently before I continue I promise you this: I'll do my best to share (some of) my romantic experiences with you, together with some of my beliefs. What you take from them, however, is entirely up to you.

A man who would be an author

Right, where do I start...? My name's Alex, I'm 30, and I live with Asperger syndrome (AS) and diabetes. I'm an anxious introspective person who's dysthymic, uncomfortable in his own skin and, oh yeah...single (form an orderly queue please, ladies).

Look a little deeper, and you might see that I am the synergistic sum of my parts. This renders me about as subtle as a brick being propelled through a closed window; on the surface it's quite amusing, but on the inside it has other connotations. It's not that I'm necessarily negative per se (although my use of grammar may indicate otherwise); I just prefer to be honest, sincere, and to the point. Some might call me a pessimist, yet I feel that's an optimistic point of view. I look at my weaknesses with a view towards improving them – what's so adverse about that? I'm rarely satisfied with my achievements, or my situation in life; I constantly feel as if there's something I should be doing, but I haven't a Scooby[1] what that something is. I firmly believe that I'll learn at least as much from writing this chapter as you will from reading it, but I'm mindful that I could forget every word I type. I suppose if I had to summarise myself in one word it would be this: conundrum.

That last word links well to the main topic of this chapter – romantic relationships. I've had a few, the 'seriousness' (for lack of a better word) of which is subjective at best. You see my AS percepts of what transpired bear no truth whatsoever; my ex-girlfriends'/dates' arguments are as equally valid. But before I get to (some of) the misdemeanours of my youth, I should start with the most important romantic relationship I've witnessed: that of my parents.

The parents beget the man-child

I can confidently state that my parents loved each other. I use the past tense because unfortunately my mum succumbed to cancer three years ago, not that she didn't put up a valiant fight before doing so. Whether they were actually in love is difficult for me to know, but if I had to choose then I'd say, 'No'. My parents (or the 'parental units', as my sisters referred to them) were together for about 29 years before Mum's passing, so it's inevitable that the dynamics of their relationship would change over that period of time. I've seen their wedding photographs and they appeared to be

---

1   Scooby-Doo = clue.

happy in them, so I suppose they must have been in love at the time.

Dad on Mum

I've never spoken to Dad about his feelings for Mum. I suspect that he too has an ASC (autistic spectrum condition), but he hasn't got a formal diagnosis. He went to a school for people with nerves (anxiety), he has his rituals and communication difficulties, and I must have got my autism genes from somewhere... Consequently, our relationship is quite strange, in that we don't talk about our feelings very much (hunger, thirst and annoyance aside). He grew up in post-war King's Cross, London, and I grew up during the Information Age in West Sussex, so apart from our mutual love of Arsenal we don't share a lot of common experiences, or interests. Nevertheless I've learnt from observation that he would always do anything for Mum, even if he didn't always execute his tasks in accordance with her matriarchal, Irish Roman Catholic will. When we moved house it was Mum's decision; Dad dutifully complied. When Granny Anne (Mum's mum) was in the final throes of dementia, he didn't object to Mum remortgaging our home so that she could help her mother with care bills. To summarise, he always bowed to Mum's resolve, although I sensed that his lack of intuition frustrated her. I think he was looking for someone to instruct and take care of him, and fortunately he found that person in Mum.

Mum on Dad

I can vaguely recall asking my Mum why she married Dad. Her response was that she found him to be 'charming'. She told me once that they had met on jury duty at Southwark Crown Court, but my recollection of the details are sketchy at best. I do know that Mum had an abusive childhood; her father used to beat both her and the rest of her family.

She left home at the age of 14, and was married to her first husband by 19. Unfortunately Mum never reconciled her differences with her father, who died ten years before my parents met. I think she was looking for someone caring with a good work ethic, and I believe that Dad has these qualities in abundance. I also think she was looking for someone she could nurture. Perhaps that's why she chose him. That said, I'll never know...

Mum versus Dad

My Mum, like her father before her, had a bit of a temper; she was also bipolar. She was always on edge, not that I necessarily blame her for that, given she had three children, and my Dad, to look after. On top of that she worked, too. Consequently when she was mad she didn't hold back. I think Dad became frustrated when Mum was frustrated; he didn't know what to do when she was angry, neither did I for that matter. I've heard it said that when people argue it shows that they care. From that perspective it would be fair to say that my parents cared – a lot. You see World War III occurred so many times in my childhood that I think I've built up a tolerance to radioactive waste (figuratively speaking). That, or I'm writing this from beyond the grave, in which case I have a spoiler alert for you people: life after death doesn't get any easier! In all seriousness, I think that if I've learnt anything from viewing my parents, then communication and compromise are prerequisites for a healthy relationship.

The man-child grows up...a little at a time

Growing up in a culture where you don't belong is bewildering at best. That's the problem with living with AS; it's there, you can feel it, but you can't necessarily express it. I wasn't diagnosed until I was 27, so traversing my infancy, youth and early adult life has been exhausting. It's only quite recently that I've been able to process what's gone on before. You see socialising takes so much time to prepare for, that I'm rarely able to get a sense of what's gone on in the past. I suppose that writing this chapter may help me towards that end. Regardless, here's the gist of my school life.

School: A bully's paradise

I always did my best to fit in at school; I really wanted to be included, especially when it came to getting a girlfriend. I used to go to school discos/parties, see my friends pairing off, and think to myself, 'I want that'. In primary school[2] I did have a few girlfriends; the mutual naïveté of youth, in terms of spending time apart, suited me. Stomach cramps (or butterflies), what I now know as a symptom of anxiety, were (and still are) omnipresent when I was (am) in the company of my peers. What didn't suit me was that it was almost entirely impossible to cover up one's shortcomings in the romance department: children see everything. If I made a mistake, such as to say something considered to be stupid (no vivid examples come to mind), then all of my classmates would know about it and (more often than not) ridicule me for my social deficiencies. I remember that on one occasion someone had written a note saying, 'Kick me', and stuck it on my back. A female friend of mine then promptly kicked me in the shin; I remember the pain vividly, both physically and emotionally.[3] I was really upset but I didn't mention it to my parents. This didn't have a direct bearing on any subsequent romantic relationships, but it certainly didn't enhance my ability (or desire) to pursue one.

Secondary school was a little different in that there was a game-changing element – hormones. My experiences of primary school verged on being egregious, so I was hopeful that a change of venue might improve my luck. In Year 7[4] I was

---

2   Elementary school in the US.

3   I suppose you can't beat the classics.

4   Grade 6 in the US.

fortunate enough to like a girl in my form who reciprocated my feelings. I was quite happy spending time with her and her friends, so on Valentine's Day I decided to buy her a present (a teddy bear, to be precise), spending about three weeks' pocket money in the process. She loved my choice of present, but later that day she decided that she didn't want to go out with me anymore. In retrospect I may have been a bit creepy in the accompanying card. I remember writing that I'd like to kiss her, but I suppose there must have been other issues that she didn't want to share with me. Needless to say, she kept the teddy!

Boy meets girl

A year later I met the first girl that I would fall in love with. She was energetic and fun to be around; she was bright and giggly, which I admired. Her domestic situation was different to mine, too, which intrigued me. What transpired was an on-again, off-again saga spanning four years, in which I must confess that I didn't treat her as well as I might have. Every time we got close, I would push her away. It felt really awkward. I remember that once we were walking to the cinema from my home and she wanted to hold my hand. I did, but it made me really uncomfortable. I'm quite hypersensitive to touch; initially it feels like a static shock, which is then carried subcutaneously from the point of contact towards my central nervous system by a colony of ants. Ironically I wasn't aware of this at the time, but given my mood swings (with puberty came the revelation that I shared Mum's temper; think the Incredible Hulk on crack cocaine and that's me at my worst) I probably wouldn't have been able to express myself adequately, anyway.

At that point I remember feeling really tired all of the time. I was still in denial about my diabetes, and as a consequence my BGs (blood glucose levels) oscillated from one extreme to another. My schoolwork suffered, and by the time I was 14 I was moved down to the second set for most of my lessons, maths and music aside. As a result I didn't really want a romantic relationship because I was so confused about the way I was feeling, but conversely I wasn't able to sufficiently explain myself to the girl I cared for; I also had a tendency to lash out at the people who cared for me. It made things awkward at school because her friends were my friends too. For a while I wasn't invited to social gatherings; I guess you could say that she won the break-up in that regard. In spite of this I still yearned for some kind of meaningful connection; I felt like there was something missing in my life. I dated a couple of girls very briefly, had my first proper kiss (wet and a bit surreal – nowhere near as good as I thought it would be), but I still didn't know what I really wanted (or needed, for that matter).

Turning point

By the time I had reached Year 11 my hormones were fully operational, especially those governed by my limbic system (not that I could make sense of them). Some of my peers were sexually active, and I was very keen to experience that first hand. There was one major problem – I wasn't sure I could trust the girl I had spent most of my teens with. She was flirting with one of our mutual friends, a guy whom her mother wanted her to marry (they would subsequently sleep together). I acknowledge that I wasn't the best person to be around, in fact let's call a spade a spade – I was a grumpy little git a lot of the time. I was keen to be seen to be mature, but inside I was completely oblivious to how I was feeling. I was aware that I was perennially tired, but couldn't explain why; I felt the ends without knowing the means.

To make matters worse, the girl's home life wasn't great.[5] Let's just say I didn't get along well with her mother, whose lifestyle choices were in stark contrast to my own. I could tell that my girlfriend was unhappy about that and I tried to

---

5   I think it'd be best to be discreet about that.

offer her pragmatic advice. At one point I even advised her to see her general practitioner (GP) to talk about depression, but she didn't listen (which, given my subsequent experience of mental health services, was probably a wise decision). By this stage we spent a fair amount of time in my bedroom, watching various TV programmes: *Friends*, *Ally McBeal* and *Match of the Day* spring to mind. It was also at around this time that I told her that I loved her; the look of shock on her face is ingrained on my mind for eternity. She didn't say anything in reply.

Roll on to the year 2000, and we decided to lose our virginity together after we had sat our GCSEs (she didn't want to be thinking about sex during the exams). We had spent a fair amount of time 'going around the bases', so to speak. I remember one night I was exploring her vulva with my finger, when my Dad walked into my room without knocking. I've never sat up so quickly in all of my life! The problem was that I still didn't trust her. The exams came and went, and then she asked me, rather bluntly: 'So, when are we going to do it, then?' I said that we weren't, and that was the end of that (or at least that's all I'm prepared to disclose).

University challenged

University brought its own set of problems. You see I grew up believing that I would have the time of my life at uni; the magic of cinema had fooled me into believing that I'd meet a girl, we'd hook up, we'd live happily ever after...you get the gist. Reality is a stark contrast, however. Surprise, surprise, I didn't have any romantic relationships whilst I studied (or to be more specific, played a lot of *Championship Manager*).

Valentine's Day Massacre II

In my first year I sent a Valentine's Day card, including a poem, to a friend whom I thought liked me. I remember a drunken night out the previous December where she seemed particularly flirty, even to my 'mind-blind' eyes.

She texted me two weeks later to say that she wasn't sure how she felt about me, which didn't surprise me (two weeks is a long time to wait for good news, right?). She left uni a couple of months later (oops, I didn't think it was that bad a poem). Her best friend at uni was also my housemate. Talk about awkward...

Drunken encounter 1: A fortunate coincidence

Fast forward ten months and I was back home for the Christmas break. I went out with some friends to catch up. I was in my default socialising mode (drunk) when I started talking to friends of friends. The next day I received a text message from an unknown number. I believe it said something like: 'Are you alright young man?' An awkward text conversation ensued, after which I recalled that whilst talking to these friends of friends (one of whom happened to be a girl) I had decided to flash her my stomach,[6] after which I told her to text me in the morning to tell me how much of a twat I'd been! My drunken whimsical state had obviously worked its charm, however, because the result of that awkward conversation was a date; my first since school.

What followed was even more difficult than the text conversation. We agreed to meet at a bar and I turned up early, as is my custom. I was so anxious that I started pacing around outside, at which point I heard someone ask me: 'Alex, are you alright?' It was my date for the evening; I didn't even recognise her in my sober state of mind! Eventually we got drinks (diet lemonade for me, I think white wine for her), after which the inquisition began with, 'So, young man, tell me a bit about yourself.' You can imagine the wind rushing between my ears when I heard that question. I can't remember what I said, but my heart remained in my ribcage, just. Abstruse open-ended lines of questioning

---

6   Whilst at school I was a half-decent sprinter, so consequently I have a reasonable physique.

leave me a gawping mess; it's in those moments that I feel like English is my second language.

The weirdest moment came at the end of the evening. You know the one, the 'Do I kiss her?' scenario. I felt like I wanted to, but I wasn't sure how to initiate it. Needless to say, my mind went blank. I remember her giving me an uncomfortable smile (or it could have been coy – I don't know), after which we agreed to meet again once she'd returned from travelling. Later that night I broke one of the unwritten rules of dating; I texted her to say that I enjoyed the evening and that I hoped she got home safe. I think she liked that, but then again I can't be certain. Incidentally we did meet again the following summer (this time for coffee), but it became clear to me that she just wanted to be friends, which we still are, in the Facebook sense of the word.

Drunken encounter 2: The text declaration
My final year at uni was tumultuous, at best. I wasn't really sure what I wanted to do with my life (still no change there), and Mum was stressed out because her mother was dying (I didn't have a clue how to help). In spite of this I grew close to a girl on my course. She was from Norway, and she thought I was intelligent (something which has never been substantiated). I was really attracted to her accent and her eyes, especially when she got frustrated. She also rivalled me in the sarcasm stakes, which was a bonus. We spent a lot of time together: walking, watching chick-flicks (I like the odd rom-com: deal with it) whilst drinking a lot of wine and eating too many crisps, just generally chatting. I felt comfortable in her presence, and I think that our mutual friends thought that we'd end up together. The problem was that she was seeing another guy at the time.

The first time I realised that she may have had feelings for me was when we were on a night out with friends to celebrate the end of the Autumn/Winter Term. She caught me completely by surprise when she said that she had been attracted to me when we had met in the first year. I was so taken aback that I didn't know how to respond. The truth was that I was attracted to her, but I think I told her that I didn't think about her in that way. I did so because she was living with a guy when we met (in case you hadn't figured it out, fidelity is important to me). Given that I was following her around uni like a lost puppy dog most of the time, I think my feelings were pretty clear, however.

About five months later it all came to a head at the end of yet another drunken night out. She didn't come because she was with her boyfriend, so I texted her declaring that I loved her, then proceeded to go home and sleep for 27 hours (which is still my personal best by some considerable margin). Needless to say that made things exceedingly uncomfortable. Again, we're still friends...on Facebook. I've come to realise that I was infatuated with her, which wasn't particularly healthy. I also feel that perhaps she just liked being thought of as attractive. Who knows?

Internet dating: A lesson in the art of bovine faeces

Shortly after my AS diagnosis, I decided that I wanted to try dating again. One in four relationships now start online, at least that's what the blurb claims, so I thought I'd give internet dating a shot. I went through the monotony of filling in my profile (contrary to what you might believe, I don't actually enjoy talking/writing about myself), found a picture of me in which I don't appear to be auditioning for a gurning competition (an arduous task), and searched for ladies based upon some arbitrary 'compatibility' algorithm. To cut a long story short, I didn't get much interest. I think that's because, unlike a lot of people who seem to want everything from life, I'm more realistic. The number of ladies who wanted to go travelling was staggering (try growing up in a foreign culture where your native language is also a foreign one – that'll cure your travel bug). Most of them wanted some form of adventure (going out for a pint of milk can put my limbic system on brown alert); they appeared to want everything they could get their hands on, without making any compromises. It was as if I stumbled across a herd of self-aggrandising cows who were oblivious to what they actually needed, and yet were fervently seeking that which was unobtainable (at least in my eyes). I suppose at least I could deduce why they were single!

It's all relative

On the face of it, it would appear that today's society is more concerned with living for the moment, than actually acknowledging it for what it is: a stage of a journey (life) in which one learns to be at peace with oneself. For instance, can you imagine what it would be like if we didn't rely on credit, if instead we actually waited until we could afford something before we decided to consume it, let alone understand its implications on our future happiness? I don't claim to be perfect. I believe that perfection is an abstract concept begotten of flawed individuals (i.e. human beings), which at best strikes me as being oxymoronic. That's why in my experience finding love – especially in a romantic context – appears to be esoteric; it's specific to the individual, so it can't be homogenised and traded.

The function of meaning

In my AS diagnostic report it states that I find relationships to be functional, rather than meaningful. I would qualify that statement by saying that without a function a relationship can't have meaning. Romance is a relatively new concept, since prior to the Victorian era most marriages were arranged, and hence love didn't necessarily play a part. That said, I am quite capable of loving someone, but as a consequence of my past experience I'm still learning to be guarded around people, especially when dealing with confrontation. That, coupled with the time it takes for me to process my thoughts and feelings, means that I will probably struggle to have a truly reciprocal relationship, period.

As I type I'm in two minds as to whether or not I want this published. On the one hand I feel that it would be good for me personally to share my thoughts and feelings; on the other I'm aware that by doing so I open myself up to criticism, and perhaps even more ridicule (or verbal abuse) from the ladies I once knew. The opportunity cost of this situation is that I can keep my anonymity by not stating my name. However, I feel that nothing worth doing is (or should be) easy, so I'm going ahead with it. If nothing else, it'll provide me with more learning opportunities.

Flexibility is key

A very famous physicist stated that for every action, there is an equal and opposite reaction. Okay, so I'm referring to Sir Isaac Newton's Third Law of Motion, but I think it can be applied to relationships, which involve the meshing of (at least) two minds (and occasionally bodies) into a semi-coherent whole (or sweaty mess). Doing so involves making choices to be flexible; to know when to give and take. Harking back to the middle-aged man, it's possible that he finds himself in his current situation because he wasn't willing or able to compromise his behaviours and beliefs in order to find someone to share his life with. Like us, he lives in a society where there's a surfeit of information and a finite amount of time to process it; consequently there's a chance that he missed something of importance. Having said that, perhaps he's happy in his current situation (after all, he's just a figment of my imagination).

To sum up, while I believe I know something of romantic relationships, I wouldn't like to state that I know where I am in relation to finding a lady with whom to share my life. I live a solipsistic existence; a state of reality that's probably incongruent with yours. I'd like to think that I'll find someone one day, but given that I spent my formative years trying to live up to the expectations of others – that my locus of identity was external – I'm currently still finding my sense of self. I'm aware that this sense of self will be compromised every time I enter a relationship, so I'm not going to be churlish enough to make a list of demands for my ideal lady. If I'm extremely fortunate then I'll find someone who I can be truly intimate with; someone who I feel able to be myself around without any repercussions. Who knows, maybe I'll even have a family of my own someday. Conversely it may well be that I read this chapter in 20 years' time and not recognise the person that I am today. You see, as the title clearly states, I'm a Man in Progress.

Chapter 4

A Marriage of Two Halves

Dr Sandra Beale-Ellis

Introduction by Luke Beardon

Sandra's chapter is a wonderful narrative full of rich experiences she has shared with the reader. A fascinating insight into the relationship between two people diagnosed as being on the autism spectrum, the writing teems with seeming contradictions – the highs of a relationship juxtaposed with some lows. In some ways it might appear that the relationship is somewhat volatile – but throughout there is a sense of absolute compassion and trust between Sandra and Joe. The way in which they have supported one another in their various (and considerable) achievements is a testimony to how strong a relationship can be between two autistic individuals. The longevity of the relationship alone is impressive; more impressive, however, is the way in which Sandra and Joe have learned together how to co-exist in a way that suits them both. Of course, it is clear that sacrifices on both sides have had to be made; what is equally clear is that the ultimate result is enviable. Sandra's writing is always a pleasure to read; her ability to be straightforward and honest shines through in this chapter, and the end result is inspirational.

My inspiration to write about our relationship on this particular day was fuelled by a busy and extremely stressful week, which ended yesterday with a double meltdown.

My over-anxious ranting caused a sudden rage in my husband. Today I am sick in one room and he is quiet and withdrawn in another. Outside the back door is a broken lamp! Our gloriously intuitive Yorkshire terriers are quietly wandering from one room to the next attempting to offer cuddles as necessary.

I know from experience, it will take a couple of days to get back to normal...or at least our normal.

Joe and I have been together for 25 years and married for 19. I am not entirely sure how we have managed that great achievement, but I do know that we love each other with an intensity many couples would envy.

We have both been given late clinical diagnoses of Asperger syndrome so it was not autism which brought us together...or was it? Diagnosis at least explained some of the behaviours we both exhibited over the years and our reactions to what happened around us.

On the face of it we met at a nightclub: I was dancing and he was a doorman watching me. This scenario definitely does not bode well for an autistic ideal: loud music, flashing lights, smoke machines and, in those days, cigarette smoke as well, people jammed against each other shouting and drinking. For me, it was an opportunity to dance which was my passion from the age of four years; and for him an opportunity to make some money and get away from his then wife who wound him up more than a little and caused many arguments, on a day-to-day basis.

It took us some months to get together; by then he had separated from his wife; feeling brave enough to realise he could have a different life. As we became an item, I had just moved to London, some 60 miles away, and he spent the first few weeks writing to me daily and bombarding me with flowers daily. It all became too much for me and I ended the relationship. Of course looking back, I realise I was probably his new special interest at that time. With a new home and a new job, a new relationship was one step too far for me.

According to him he went into a deep depression and gave up on his life to start again in a tiny flat and get away from all the memories. Several weeks after we split up, I realised I missed him and we eventually got back together after a couple of months and I moved back from London into the tiny flat.

Our relationship was never easy from the start; he would fly into rages and I never understood why. His ex-wife told me we would never last six months; whether it was to prove her wrong I am not sure, but I was determined we would last and we got engaged after seven months together. We had some fantastic times. He was so caring and wanted to look after me. We moved into a new flat some months later and life moved on.

Joe was always very insistent that I made the most of my skills; he was never happy with me simply being a medical secretary; he thought I deserved more. I loved my job; I enjoyed the medical environment, I am a perfectionist, loving paperwork and organising things and people. Whilst I was still working, he encouraged me to start a little business typing manuscripts and other small jobs. I even won a Prince of Wales Youth Business Award. We then set up an organisation together, which is still running today and to date has over 50,000 members. He also encouraged me to take a teaching course, again while I worked full time. As I have since completed a doctorate in education, I guess you could say he was my motivation and inspiration. Alternatively I like to think he is just pushy and I concede I sometimes need a good kick to get me going (metaphorically that is).

We have supported each other in our careers and both have very public personas in our various areas. In private things are quite different. Few people know exactly what goes on behind the doors to our beautiful home in the country.

I love to be his wife; I enjoy at times a 40s-style relationship with my husband. I am intelligent, successful and independent but I love to look after him. I always take him a cup of tea in bed in the morning; I cook almost every night; I do the laundry and love to do housework. I enjoy choosing gifts for him at birthdays and Christmas. This is not for one moment a one-sided relationship though. He will bring me tea in bed, always has a cuppa ready for me if I have been out and obsesses over cleaning the kitchen sink! He will go out for a day and always bring me back a little gift. He still looks after me as he did when we first got together. Together we have concreted, built, paved, painted, shovelled and scrubbed; we have built our various homes to be where we are now through working together, not always in complete harmony, but with persistence and love.

Over the years the rages have subsided but they still occur usually when Joe is tired or hungry, or something externally has wound him up to the extent he just loses control. We no longer have holes in walls but the occasional accident will occur. It probably doesn't help that we work together during the day and often together in the evening as well. If I am feeling overwhelmed I can get snappy and stroppy which may cause him to react.

I have extreme anxieties which I originally thought were related to his behaviours. However, after taking time over the years to contemplate this, I realise I was always an anxious person. I compensated by controlling everything and everyone around me. Even when I was very ill as a child, I used to boss my parents around and would never let a doctor or nurse touch me unless I knew exactly what, why, how...

Over the years we have learned to fit together like hand in glove. I would put systems into place to ensure Joe could not find a reason to be upset. Keys, wallet, pens, whatever would all have specific places; if keys, for example, went missing and he was having a bad day, my day would certainly be spoilt as well. When I get overwhelmed or anxious, I tend to clean and tidy and this in turn keeps him calm. His behaviours have allowed me to feed my own controlling needs.

He often says that we are complete opposites and we probably shouldn't be together. For many reasons he is probably right. His snoring drives me insane, and I have woken him on more than a few occasions with my chatting in my sleep. He hates the feel of my hair on his skin and my breath as well. In bed, I have to put the duvet up over my mouth so that my breathing doesn't bother him.

I look forward to occasions when he will go away overnight; just to feel peaceful and not on edge, wondering what will happen next. But after a night or two, I miss him like crazy and get excited about him coming home again.

He is very romantic at times; he will choose greetings cards very carefully for example, ensuring the words are just right. He never forgets my birthday or our anniversary and will always have thought carefully about the gift. He will take me out for meals and surprise me with little love tokens whenever the mood takes him. We still leave each other little love notes.

On other occasions he has no idea. Our wedding day for example, after the main reception, when we should have been retiring to our room in the beautiful country house hotel in which we were married, he chose to invite our families to sing around the fire for hours and hours, and then to come up and take a look in our room. I can't remember what time they all left that room but let's say the wedding night was not what I expected!

Somehow, though, we just fit together; we complement each other. We love to go to the cinema and sit hand in hand in the same seats each time, every now and again just looking at each other and knowing what the other is feeling or thinking. We tease each other relentlessly in public but never argue at home. If we disagree or feel like shouting at each other, one of us will usually leave the room and get space elsewhere. We have our own private rooms – his for relaxing with his music and computer, mine my study where I write, plan or read. Sometimes we separate for hours at a time but that space between us allows us to survive such a long-term relationship with the sometimes challenging issues autism brings to us.

But I couldn't imagine my life without Joe and I am not sure he could imagine his without me. If you ask our dogs about us you might just get a different story...

For now, then, we remain separated in our two rooms, recovering from the traumatic episode that was yesterday, and eventually we will gradually move towards each other and continue our lives in our own unique way.

Chapter 5

Learning to Adapt to a Different Type of Relationship

Joseph Edmonds

Introduction by Luke Beardon

This is an absolutely compelling read. Tragic in parts and uplifting in others, Joseph gives an extremely honest and insightful portrayal of his experiences and ongoing issues with relationships. In a relatively few number of words he manages to convey a whole host of areas that are pertinent to him, which provide an excellent insight into just some of the problems that a person on the spectrum might face. He describes brilliantly how he struggles to fit in with what is deemed socially conventional, and the impact that this has had on his life. Joseph makes some pertinent comments about how being himself has potentially disadvantaged him – and yet puts forward the persuasive argument that it is essentially his right to be who he is, and not being the same as the majority does not make him somehow inferior. As he states towards the end of the chapter, he needs to be allowed, and accepted, for who he is.

Introduction

My name is Joseph Edmonds. I'm 46 years old and, although I've not yet sought an official identification, I attended Luke Beardon's talk on Autism and Anxiety in July 2014, and I believe that I have Asperger syndrome (AS).

Young and lonely

In 1992, at the age of 24, I still hadn't had any kind of romantic relationship. All throughout my teens, I'd felt that I was missing out on so much. I'd never socialised in the evenings with anyone from school or college, and found it easier to stay at home. I'd always kept people at arms length, to avoid the inevitable hurt and upset that came when I tried to relax and be myself around others.

In some ways, my life at that time was going well. Despite finding mainstream school and college quite traumatic, life as an adult was easier, as I had more control over what I did. I'd learnt to drive when I was 17, and had performed well academically in maths and science, winning the course attainment prize at college – although I was too scared to collect it. So as a relatively young adult, I'd ended up with a fairly good job as an electronics engineer.

When I first tried going out at night, my Dad told me not to expect too much. That advice didn't sit well with me – I didn't like the idea of setting my sights too low. I was quite hard on myself, often wondering what was wrong with me. I couldn't understand how other people were having relationships, whereas I'd not got anywhere at all. Some people thought I was gay, even when I was at school – that was the default assumption about anyone who was different in any way. Others thought that I was very shy, or just odd. I didn't have anyone who was even close to being a real friend.

When I was about 20, my Dad became ill. That contributed to a change in my behaviour, and I made more of an effort to try new things. For most of my life, my Dad had been like a best friend to me. He was relatively old – he was nearly 49 when I was born, and had been in World War II. Having older parents was yet another thing that made me different. My Dad had never learnt to drive, and seemed remarkably content with few possessions. We used to go cycling together at the weekends, until I got my first car. He took an interest in everything I did and, apart from my childhood problems with temper, and having fewer material things compared to other children, I'd generally felt happy at home.

For a while, I used to go to a local pub every Saturday night, where a DJ played records. Attractive women called in for drinks, on their way to nightclubs. But I was self-conscious about my appearance, and didn't dare approach them. An older drunken lady once talked to me, and asked why I was alone. I felt embarrassed and left. On another occasion, I went to a singles night, but was far younger than anyone else – so I soon left.

Every Sunday night, I used to listen to a radio programme that played soul music. The DJ also played records every month in a nearby city. After some sleepless nights, I decided to get some contact lenses and better clothes, and give it a try! I worried about getting lost, so I went during the daytime – I must have driven around the city ten times! When the evening came, I returned there, but failed to have a conversation with anyone. The music was loud, and I struggled to hear what most people were saying. One of the regulars asked me 'Why are you here on your own? Where are all your friends?' I just wanted a hole to appear beneath me, so I could disappear! That was the one and only time I went there.

In 1990, when I was 22, my Dad died. Losing him hit me really hard. I got no support from my Mum or two older sisters – they appeared to think I was totally devoid of emotion. In reality, nothing could have been further from the truth. That gave me another big push to try something different.

I was interested in electronics, computers, music and cars – things that I could do alone. I used to go to town every weekend, and buy books and magazines. I felt attracted to the young woman who usually served me, but worried about my age – she was probably 18 and I was 23. After a few sleepless nights, I decided to do something about it, but felt unable to speak to her directly – so I wrote her a letter instead. The next Saturday morning, I arrived early, and waited outside the shop, nervously holding the letter and a bunch of flowers. I felt rather conspicuous, and my anxiety level increased as shop workers started to arrive at the mall. But just for once, she didn't turn up for work! So I disposed of the flowers and letter, and didn't try again. I didn't tell anyone about that for at least 20 years.

First relationship

After failing with the shop assistant, life seemed bleak, and I'd pretty much given up on the idea of finding a girlfriend at that point. I used to read the want ads in the local papers, partly for fun, but also daydreaming a little bit. In August 1992 one of the ads caught my attention. It began with the words 'Quiet, shy female.' I imagined that it might be someone more like me. It seemed much more genuine than the others. So after sweating about it for a night, I decided to reply. As always, I didn't confide in anyone about what I'd done.

I received a response, and although terrified, I managed to phone up and arrange for us to meet that Friday evening. When the evening arrived, I was so nervous that I wore the wrong shirt! I had two similar ones, but one was ripped. I'd ironed the good one, and ended up wearing the bad one!

I decided to stop worrying about things like my glasses and crooked teeth. Instead, I decided to make a huge effort to talk, and appear 'normal, friendly and interesting'. It took all the energy I had, but Jane and I got along really well. We talked all night, and arranged to see each other the following day. Apart from day four, we saw each other every day from then on! The months that followed were wonderful. I was finally doing the things that others of my age had been doing for years!

Looking back, most major life changes for me have started with a growing feeling of dissatisfaction, followed by a period where a pressure builds up inside me. Then something happens to tip me over the edge – an extra push that makes me take a risk. Sadly, despite some very successful outcomes, I often focus on the failures, or potential failures.

After meeting Jane, things moved rapidly. By November 1992 we were searching for a house. In December, we got engaged. We purchased a house in May 1993 and got married in January 1994. It was a small, quiet wedding. At our wedding reception, despite being very nervous, I managed to give what I think was a reasonable speech. A little later, everyone – including Jane – was sitting around chatting in small groups. I found myself on my own, so I walked around and tried talking to a few people, but failed to get anyone's attention. I suddenly felt very lonely and isolated – like I was different to everyone else. It also made me angry – this was my wedding – and it felt like I was being ignored by everyone, including Jane. That played on my mind for quite some time afterwards.

Just the two of us

Unlike me, Jane initially had a couple of friends. One was someone who she used to work with. They'd been on holiday together, and occasionally went to the cinema. Jane's other friend was from a non-religious church group. She was also a witness at our wedding. I remember her coming to our house for a chat, which was a new and pleasant experience for me. I was always nervous about anyone coming to see us, but it also felt good to be doing something 'normal'.

At this point, you need to know that I have to make a big effort to smile and for my face to appear friendly – my default expression makes me appear standoffish.

When Jane's friend was chatting, I remember her saying something surprising, and I think my expression made her feel unwelcome. That wasn't what I wanted at all. Sadly, she never came to our house again, and later moved away from the area.

I'd imagined that my social circle might expand through Jane, but I was somewhat surprised when she let her friendships fade, and spent all her time with me. It wasn't what I'd expected, but I loved being the only one that she needed. We were everything to each other. We didn't need anyone else.

Apart from the fact that we didn't socialise with other couples, and only rarely went to social events, it felt like we had a fairly normal life. We both worked. She enjoyed things like reading, needlecraft and baking. I enjoyed music, electronics and computers. We both liked sci-fi and had a similar sense of humour. I did a lot of DIY on the house, and Jane helped me with much of that too.

We loved each other, and loved spending time together – we could be ourselves, without fear of what the other one would say or think. We could be silly or childish at times, just for fun. Everything was accepted – there were no barriers. Perhaps we weren't like other couples, but we were happy. There was no question about whether we would stay together – we were right for each other, and could have happily spent the rest of our lives together.

Open University

Neither of us had gone to university, so we both did OU degrees. That was convenient, as we worked full time. The tutorials were popular with most students, but Jane and I avoided them wherever possible! I didn't like trying to interact with tutors and other students.

Our OU degrees included one-week residential courses. In 1996 we stayed in different buildings, but spent the evenings together, rather than with other students. In 1999 we went on separate weeks. We'd never been apart for that long before and, after I dropped Jane off at the station, I was in a terrible state. It felt like she'd left me forever, and it took hours for me to calm down.

Children

By choice, we remained childless until 2005, when we had our first son. Just one year later our second son was born. Jane had a retained placenta, and had to have surgery to remove it. I was left alone for an hour or so with our newborn child. I remember being terrified that something might happen to her. The thought of living without her was unbearable, as was the idea of caring for two children on my own. I was so relieved to see her in the recovery room!

Having children meant that we had less time for each other, which put some pressure on us. Then Jane had an early miscarriage in 2007, which started a period of depression for her. In addition, I got a different job, and moved from a tiny local company, where I'd worked for 20 years, to a larger company farther away from home, where things were completely different. Despite those pressures, we remained close.

After having children, Jane became friends with other mums. However, I didn't become friends with other dads. For me, that highlighted some differences between us. Most of the time, I didn't really care – I didn't have time for them, and we had little in common. But I felt awkward at children's parties and school events, where it seemed that I was expected to talk to other parents – like everyone else was doing.

Devastating news

In 2010 everything changed in a devastating and unexpected way. Jane was diagnosed with breast cancer. It had already spread to her spine – so it was incurable. Things seemed very bleak initially, but the first round of treatments helped, and I was amazed that she was soon back on her feet. She even returned to work briefly! It's hard to believe it now, but we seemed to carry on as before, pretending that everything was going to be alright.

After Jane became ill, one of the school mums wrote her a lovely letter, offering to take her out and help with housework. At first, Jane put it to one side. But I encouraged her to accept and develop other friendships. The scale of Jane's health problems made me realise that we couldn't do everything alone. I remember saying to her 'You can't let people like that slip through your fingers.' I did feel pangs of jealousy once or twice, even though she was only going out with some female friends. It felt like I was no longer needed, surplus to requirements or had failed to provide everything that she needed. But I knew that it made her feel better – she could forget about being ill for a while. So I continued to encourage it.

The doctors could only attempt to slow the disease down and, a few months later, more treatment was needed. Despite that, we managed to have our first family holiday in 2011. Jane was retired on ill health grounds that year, which terrified me – because they didn't think she'd ever return to work. Everyone else was simply happy that she no longer had to worry about work, and thought I was reading too much into things. Jane always asked for the prognosis to be left out of her copies of correspondence.

Things got worse again in 2012 and, by the end of the year, there were also concerns about her liver. In March 2013, when she turned 45, they confirmed that the cancer had spread there. A month later I was present when the doctors said that nothing more could be done. Watching a doctor say that to the person that means everything to you is the most awful thing imaginable.

It was the worst period of my life. Although Jane didn't want a prognosis, I got bad vibes from the nurses when she was staying at the hospice in May 2013. When I asked a doctor, he said that she had 2–12 weeks left to live! So, despite them expecting her to stay there and wait to die, I took her home. We did a few things that she wanted to do, including seeing the latest *Star Trek* film – she'd seen all the others.

Jane and I didn't talk much about what might happen to her – it was too upsetting. I couldn't stand the idea of life without her.

In June 2013 I saw her walk downstairs at home for the last time, looking truly frightened that she might fall. She ended up back in the hospice, so they could keep an eye on her for a few days whilst they arranged for a scan – they suspected that the cancer had also spread to her brain.

Things suddenly got much worse and, despite there being plans for her to come home again, I ended up staying at the hospice for a few nights.

I was alone in the room with her when she took her last breath on 12 June 2013.

Little did I know that – about one year later – I would attend a talk by Dr Luke Beardon on Autism and Anxiety. There, he would describe a situation in which someone had just one close friend, upon whom they depended for everything. And he would ask, what would happen if that person were to fall off the face of the earth?

I was about to find out...

Alone again

I had lost everything in one go. The best friend I've ever had, the one person that completed me – my whole world. Jane and I had expected to grow old together, and watch our children grow up.

But it was not to be. And, apart from my children, it left me all alone once again. I was suddenly a single dad.

As if grieving for Jane wasn't bad enough, I also had to worry about it being up to me, and me alone, to interact with other parents at the school. Those thoughts filled me with anxiety. Nobody understood quite how difficult those things were for me.

For the last two years, I've had less contact than usual with other adults – I gave up work in 2012 to look after Jane, and I'm still not ready to return. Shortly after losing her, one of her friends kindly invited me out for coffee. She's a good listener, and it helped enormously. I'd hoped that it might happen more than once, but it now looks like it was just a one-off. Perhaps what I thought was sympathy and understanding was really just pity. Jane had told me that she'd asked a few of her friends to keep an eye on me, if anything should happen to her. That was upsetting to hear. But sadly, they seem to have faded into the background, and I rarely speak to any of them now.

New start

The hospice offered me bereavement counselling, which I accepted. In August 2013 my counsellor told me about a support group for widowed people. I imagined that it would be like a movie scene, where people stand up to tell their story to the group – not my sort of thing at all!

I've never had any difficulty being alone for several hours, either at work or home. But I didn't like feeling completely isolated, with so few adults to talk to. So I took the risk and joined the support group. Fortunately, it wasn't like I'd imagined!

In order to communicate with other group members, I had to join Facebook. So in a short space of time, I was doing quite a few things that were new to me. Losing Jane had pushed me into making new attempts at socialising – rather like my Dad's death had influenced me in the early 1990s.

Over the years I've got better at putting on a good act – almost convincing myself that I can fit in. But my confidence is fragile, and I take failures to heart and dwell on them. Even if things do go well, I still need quiet time to process my experiences, and get my energy back. It's as though I have a protective skin that can cope remarkably well with a certain amount of banter and conflict. But once something has broken through, the emotional damage that follows can be long-lasting.

In social situations, my poor memory and general knowledge can make me appear stupid. I struggle to remember names and stories, particularly when I'm stressed. So I'm cautious about asking questions or using people's names, in case they make insensitive comments when I get things wrong.

Despite some reservations, I threw caution to the wind, and once again put all my energy into appearing 'normal' – rather like I'd done when I met Jane. To my surprise, I became friends with the first member of the support group that I met. Louise and I kept meeting up for coffee, and got along really well. Just making a real friend was a big thing for me. As a young child, I once referred to someone as a friend, and they immediately denied it. Since then, I've rarely felt that I have the right to describe anyone as a friend.

I've found group meals more stressful than meeting just one or two people – I often fail to be heard. Afterwards, I'm often disappointed that I've struggled to make any new friends – whereas everyone else seems to post on Facebook about what a fantastic time they've had. Reading things like that gets me down for quite some time afterwards.

More than friends

I went to Louise's birthday party in fancy dress – something new for me. I felt like I had nothing to lose – as though the costume was protecting me. Although my feelings for Louise continued to grow, I tried to keep telling myself that it was too soon after losing Jane for us to be anything more than just friends. Immediately after I'd lost Jane, I'd said that there could never be anyone else – that nobody could take Jane's place.

In November, another widow was very friendly towards me. That boosted my confidence, and we had a meal together. It took me by surprise when she wanted to be more than just friends. I'd never been in that situation before, and I didn't know what to do. At the same time, Louise joined a Facebook group for widowed dating, so I thought that there was no longer any possibility of a relationship with her. I secretly felt very upset about that, but still tried to support her.

There was a glimmer of hope when I heard stories that made me think Louise might be interested in me. After a couple of stressful days thinking about things, I told the other widow that I wanted to be with Louise. I felt terrible for hurting her feelings. When I admitted to Louise about how I felt, I was overjoyed when she felt the same way. It turned out that Louise had joined the dating group just for advice about her feelings for me! Although neither of us had been looking initially, we ended up starting a romantic relationship.

Differences

My relationship with Louise is very different to the one I had with Jane. Neither of us wants to replace the one we lost – that's impossible. But although things can't be the same, they can be just as good in different ways. It's dangerous to compare relationships, but the differences are teaching me quite a lot about myself.

My relationship with Louise is new and exciting – I'm experiencing a different side to life. However, some differences have caused difficulties, and I'm still trying to adjust. Although I soon felt relaxed around Louise, there is still a tendency for me to be nervous about expressing my wishes, and there are still a few more barriers left to come down.

Louise is more outgoing, has more friends and uses Facebook frequently. Jane didn't use Facebook at all. Thinking about it now, I sometimes wonder if Jane might have had high-functioning AS – she was more like me, especially before we had children. She was happy to stay in, and had little contact with the outside world other than work and immediate family.

Facebook

Without Facebook, I would never have met Louise. She's used it for years, and goes on there several times a day – from first thing in the morning to last thing at night. Almost everything we do, everywhere we go, it all seems to get posted on Facebook – even while we're on holiday.

Facebook gives me mixed feelings. I feel like I've got to be on there, because it's a significant part of Louise's day-to-day life, and I want to be with her in every way. But sometimes it's too intrusive – I wish we could have some days without other people being involved, in a virtual sense. Some time ago, I deactivated my account for three weeks, but ended up returning. I often feel like a bystander when online – as in real life. But it didn't feel good knowing even less about what was happening.

It's strange for me to see how Louise remains in touch with many people from her school and college days via Facebook, whereas Jane and I lost touch with pretty much everyone from the past.

I had trust issues at first, due to Louise's frequent Facebook posts, comments and messages. For her, that was normal behaviour. For me it was something completely alien, and I couldn't understand the purpose of all that activity. In contrast, Jane used to leave her phone switched off. Even in the last few years, she only sent one or two messages per week.

Sometimes Louise has said that she's been too busy to message me, despite finding time to comment on several Facebook posts. Things like that can make me feel unimportant, and get me down for some time afterwards. The fact that she often messages other people whilst I'm with her doesn't help either. We do spend a lot of time together though, so I'm trying to remember that her other friends need some attention too.

When Facebook gets me down, it helps for me to keep busy doing something that interests me – but it can be hard to ignore my feelings if I'm upset.

Friends

Although Louise has many friends, we've spent most daytimes together so far – so things have been quite intense. We both have children, and rarely go out at night. In contrast, Jane and I worked full time initially, and only spent weekends and evenings together, very rarely seeing anyone else. Occasionally, Louise has a girls' night out or a coffee morning without me, which makes me feel a bit left out. To Louise, there's nothing unusual about what she's doing, so she struggles to understand my feelings. And although she doesn't mind if I go out without her, that's not really an option – I have few friends, and I find it quite taxing.

It helps greatly if Louise tells me well in advance about plans to go out without me. If I only find out at the last minute, it causes more emotional distress. When I was ill for a few days, Louise immediately arranged to go out all day with a friend, which made me feel jealous and upset – almost abandoned, especially when she didn't contact me all day, and posted on Facebook about what a lovely time she was having. Things like that cause hours of rumination for me – I really struggle to prevent those feelings from taking over. It's difficult for me to discuss such feelings with her – I worry that it sounds like I'm trying to stop her doing what she enjoys – which is not my aim, because I'm happy to see that she's happy. I just wish it didn't make me feel bad.

Perhaps I envy Louise for her friends and social skills. The situations that I struggle with are quite new and different for me – Jane never did these things, apart from an occasional coffee morning in the last few years. In a sense, being with Louise is a constant reminder of how different I really am, which can be hard at times. Making progress at coping with these new feelings is very hard.

Despite me writing mainly about the difficulties that I've faced, Louise is fast becoming my whole world – like Jane was – and I can't imagine my life without her in it. But her need for other friends – although understandable – can still make me feel insecure, and doubt my position in her world. I worry that we might never be quite as close as I'd like, and that she'll sometimes turn to friends or Facebook, to discuss things that Jane would have shared only with me. Occasionally, when I feel down, I imagine that Louise might be better off with someone who is neurotypical (NT) – someone more like herself.

Should I change?

It hurts to think that I will never have the natural social skills of NTs – I can't change how my brain is wired. In particular, it hurts when other people make patronising statements, by saying that it's not something I'm good at, or it's not for me – especially after I've been trying hard.

Now that I've seen a different kind of life, part of me wants to be more socially active. On the other hand, I struggle to find the time or energy to maintain even one friendship, let alone multiple friendships. I also wonder about the benefit of all these friendships anyway – all the small talk seems a bit pointless. So perhaps I don't really want to change. After all, I've got this far without lots of friends!

It upsets me that there's an assumption that the NT way is the right way, and that my preference for quieter activities is not just different, but that it's wrong. There's an implication that I should be the one who adjusts, and learns to be more like NTs.

There's a dilemma over me staying in the support group. I really only remain a member because of Louise. Unlike most others, I've struggled to make friends there. In a sense, I feel trapped – if I leave the group, I'm no longer part of something that's a significant part of Louise's life, and I wouldn't be able to accompany her to group events, which troubles me greatly.

Since we've been together, I've put my interests aside, such as electronic design and making music, to be with her. When I've tried to pursue my interests, she didn't like being left on her own, and we missed each other. Also, I was anxious about her doing things without me, and couldn't concentrate on anything anyway. Therefore, I've tended to give in and always see her when possible. But I know things can't continue that way.

Lately, Louise wants to spend more time with friends and family. So I'm finally starting to get some time to myself – but not necessarily on days that suit me. However, I find it hard to decide which of my interests to pursue – which is something that's been a lifelong problem for me. Whenever I start doing one thing, it quickly feels like I should be doing something else instead. And I really do worry that this might be the start of a diverging path in my relationship with Louise.

Conclusion

My new relationship means that my life has more love, more joy, and more happiness – as well as more anxiety and worry. Fortunately, the good very much outweighs the bad – although I'm still learning to deal with negative feelings.

A romantic relationship between someone with AS/ autism spectrum disorder and someone who is NT needs understanding and compromise on both sides – and those things require good, honest communication. Finding a balance that works for both people takes time, but will be worth the effort.

For me, a romantic relationship is an all-or-nothing thing. It can't work unless my partner is also my best friend. I need to be accepted for who I am. I need to be allowed to be myself. It's so important that I feel understood, as well as loved. In general, my life is improving again, and I truly hope that things work out with my new relationship.

Chapter 6

True Love, Finding Someone Special Enough to Deserve Me

Lynette Marshall

Introduction by Luke Beardon

This is such an uplifting chapter written by someone who has a wonderful outlook on life. It is fantastic that she has found herself in a positive relationship, and she makes no excuses for being herself. Of course, it is not easy for everyone to simply be themselves and expect a relationship to come their way – but Lynette demonstrates very well that, for her, being her true self in the long term has proven to be a positive step.

Dedicated to my partner David Barnes

I used to think that I was the world's worst at relationships. I also used to think that the hardships that I felt regarding relationships were unique to me because I have Asperger syndrome (AS). Until I got a bit older and realised that rejection, hurt and disappointment are felt by everybody at some time in their lives. They are not feelings that are experienced because you have got autism or because you have not got autism but simply because it is not humanly possible for every person who you like romantically to share those same feelings. Hence, people are inevitably hurt. It is just that our feelings may express themselves in very different ways.

The way that I see my past experiences now is that those relationships were practices for my relationship that I would have with someone who truly deserves me, my current partner. Though everybody has disagreements, the same AS traits that past men picked fault with are the same traits that my partner loves about me. It is a matter of finding the right person to fit with you. In my experience finding the right person was not easy but was well worth the wait. Nobody should have to put on an act in an intimate relationship and indeed an act could not be maintained in the long run. Everybody is special and there is no better feeling than finding someone who loves you just the way you are. I think that it is useful to try and find somebody who is sensitive, who understands autism or who is prepared to understand people's differences. Also, a person with AS can have a lot to offer a relationship. They can be highly trustworthy, loyal and honest. I felt that a big issue within relationships was how soon to tell a prospective partner that I have AS. My thoughts were – how soon is too soon? What if it puts them off? What if they get scared because they do not understand AS? I still do not know the answer to how soon to tell a prospective partner. I think that it depends on the individual situation and also when a relationship develops is when you learn more about each other anyway. It is impossible to take the autism out of us and so our traits will surface anyway.

If a relationship fails don't blame yourself. My view is that if they don't love you for who you are then they are either not worth it or you won't be as happy as you could be with someone else. If they do love you and you love them then you have found somebody really special. I never believed that a relationship would happen for me. People said that I should stop looking for a man and one day he would be right there. I am now four years into a long-term relationship and I could not be happier. I fully intend to marry the man I love and have children one day. Those that know me know that I won't let AS stop me from doing anything. In fact I rarely stop to consciously think about the fact that I do have AS anymore. I am so busy with just being me! Though, from time to time I have heard some comments that have angered me. I was at a conference on autism once when somebody said that 'people with autism could not enjoy a sexual life' and I was quite appalled. Having a sexual life is something which I consider to be a private matter and at the choice of the individuals concerned whether they engage in sexual activity or not. But it certainly is not something which people with AS cannot experience or cannot enjoy. It might be true that some people with AS may want to be single, preferring their own company. Of course, this is absolutely fine! But I know from experience that many people with AS want similar things in life to people who are neurotypical (NT). They speak of having their own house, marrying and having children one day. As a person in a happy, stable relationship who does not wish to go into too much private detail, I write this chapter mainly to help others to benefit from the mistakes that I have made along the way.

Here are my tips:

- Love yourself. Be happy with you. You will then shine to others.

- Personally I would avoid internet dating as there are some people who are not very nice out there. I do accept that the use of a computer in making friendships may be preferred to those with AS so if you are determined to try internet dating follow the next step.

- At the least, whether internet dating or not, always tell a family member or close friend where you are

going to if arranging to meet up, when you plan to
be back and take your mobile phone (with credit and
charged) along with you. The best of friendships and
relationships can develop over time and so take time
to get to know anybody new.

- Try not to be so keen on finding a relationship that
  you accept poor treatment. A good relationship is
  about respect and a person should treat you nicely.

- Remember that it is not a running race. Keep to a
  pace that is good for your partner as well as yourself.
  'I love you' and marriage will not come overnight.

- It is healthy to spend time apart. Having your own
  friends and interests are a good thing.

- Once in a long-term relationship, try to keep talking.
  If speech is difficult write a note!

Since being in a stable, loving relationship I have felt more
positive about my life in general. Happiness is the most
important thing. Whilst I wish you all to find the same level
of happiness that I have, remember that if your happiness
comes from being single that is also good. If you are single
but would like to be in a relationship, be yourself but have
patience.

Having AS certainly will not stop me from being a great wife
and mother. Good luck.

Love to all,

Lynette x

Chapter 7

Benefits and Drawbacks of Relationships in a Different Culture to One's Own

Freddie

Introduction by Dean Worton

I honestly thought that 50 years ago, it was actually quite rare for anyone to be single, no matter how awkward. Nevertheless, it seems that there have always been problems for people who today would be diagnosed with Asperger syndrome (AS) or autism. It would be interesting to learn whether someone discovering their AS/autism can actually help them towards having romantic relationships should they seek them out. One thing I've often thought is that when someone with AS acts in a socially awkward way it is more likely to be due to lack of knowledge of social techniques and what to say at what time and in what situation than simply what is often unhelpfully classed as 'shyness'.

It is also interesting taking a look at how living and loving in a country foreign to the AS individual could work out. There are indeed the inevitable language barriers unless the language is studied. Cultural barriers are always going to exist even for predominant neurotype (PNT) individuals, so will be greater for people with AS, but as Freddie suggests there is always capacity to hide behind our perceived 'foreigness' when acting in an autistic way. I doubt it will work every time if the autism is quite severe but, where symptoms are milder, it could just be taken as 'Are all Brits this way?', and as AS/autism are not widely recognised in some countries, the foreign partner might not think there is anything fundamentally different with their partner.

As a teenager growing up in the 1960s, romance didn't really come naturally to me, so I hardly ever pursued it. I suppose there were some weak vestigial elements of attraction and social pressure coming into play, but I didn't really get into romance very much as a teenager because I didn't know what it was or how to get into it. It wasn't until beyond my teens in my 20s that I could experience anything that you could call romantic. I eventually felt I was missing out on what others were doing so thought I'd better try and associate with a member of the opposite sex. Although I took a girl I knew out quite a bit and we did a few things together I had no idea what I should be doing to turn it into a relationship and it's doubtful whether it qualified as a relationship at all.

As soon as I was diagnosed, I started to look at relationships in more detail. If during my teenage years I had known that I had AS, I would have studied relationships in more detail and I might have actually achieved some romance while I was still a teenager since I wouldn't have been dwelling so much on why I was different; I would probably have been more relaxed and natural.

In those days, there weren't many particular advantages for male Aspie teens in my experience compared to today, but I didn't waste time or concern myself with relationship issues and concentrated on other interests and studies instead. I was in the dark as to why I was different to others, and wrongly thought of it as a personal weakness, which made me less confident of myself, less assertive, and more introverted than I need have been. I believe that relationships have always been difficult for Aspies, and I would query the concept that it's 'increasingly' difficult today. I don't think unless Aspies are given examples to follow, and are taught what they are supposed to do that they can just do it as a natural thing because we tend to suppress our own natural inclinations.

Having AS certainly made it harder to know what to do in a relationship and harder to anticipate the expectations of a female partner. One could look at films and read books but I didn't relate those to reality. They were just fiction and I didn't see any direct link between what I saw in films and books and me as a real person, so it was very difficult. I had no idea what to do, and could only fall back on trying to be polite and cooperative as I'd been taught to do as a young child by my grandparents, and being nice to female partners, but this all lacked being natural. In retrospect, this wasn't enough for a female partner. A female partner probably expected a more natural, impulsive and human approach (like a PNT without any inhibitions) instead of me being all tensed up trying to be nice to them. I would advise readers, 'Don't think about what you're doing. Just do what you want to do.' I know, from my point of view, I was far too inhibited to go anywhere near that.

If I'd been aware of my AS sooner, I'd have addressed the relationship problem much earlier and I'd have used that knowledge to study relationships and perfect them much better. I'd have had a better chance of finding meaningful relationships and consequently would have gained more experience in handling them, and in that way I'd have become far better equipped to maintain such relationships.

In my early relationships and early married life I liked the economy of scale in shopping, cooking, driving around in a car and organising somewhere to live for two people compared to one on his own. I was lonely on my own and

I lacked the certain satisfaction out of doing things which please other people. I least liked unexpectedly becoming the father to a child, and this is a strong and sore point with me. I didn't like having to bend to what the partner liked to do all the time, although I did feel an obligation to do that bending, so in some ways I lost myself because I didn't get time to do my own things. Another thing I didn't like was my new wife weeping a lot soon after we were married and her being unwilling or unable to explain what was wrong. When I asked, she said 'You ought to know', but I really didn't know. This went on for a long time, I found it distressing and didn't like that at all.

I suppose partners were expecting me to be more PNT-like and more natural but I wasn't able to do that. I believed I was being the ideal husband as I'd been brought up to be. I paid for the accommodation and paid the weekly housekeeping. We went out and did things together but I fell short somehow or other; I didn't really know how, but in some way I didn't behave naturally, the way a more normal human being would. Looking back on it now with a little more knowledge and experience of what relationships are supposed to be all about, I'd say I failed to enter into a really loving two-way relationship with my new wife. We were busy attending to the mechanics of our new life and concentrated on this new experience rather than on appreciating each other's presence. We were living our life. I was going to work, commuting, and I would come home and eat my dinner and we would do things in the house that needed doing but we were lacking intimate dialogue and understanding of each other's wants and needs. We did what we thought was right but it wasn't natural. We soon took each other for granted instead of feeling any need for romance.

In being a couple, I did enjoy the economies of scale in general living such as sharing a house, a car, and feeling justified doing things that would have felt too extravagant if I'd undertaken them as a single person. 'I'm a mean old beggar normally on my own.' I enjoyed being welcomed at social events as a couple and allowing my partner to do some of the talking for both of us instead of me having to do it all by myself. Above all else, I became very upset about having an unwanted child. Also feeling an obligation to accompany and spend time doing boring things that my partner enjoyed, and having to cut short or completely cut out time spent following my own eccentric interests because my partner found them boring.

If I had a choice of what ratio of my leisure time would be spent around my partner and how much time alone, very different answers apply to different phases of my marriages and different partners. When I first married, I felt an obligation to spend all my spare time together with my wife. I thought it was my duty for us to be a couple and do everything together, but that marriage didn't succeed in the long run. With my much longer-surviving second marriage to a foreign wife with a foreign culture, we are deliberately distant with the ratio of time spent together down to five per cent or less and 95 per cent on our own. I'm not saying that one ratio is better than the other, but the one where we are more separate is so far lasting longer.

Much of the year, I have a long-distance marriage. The advantages of this are that absence makes the heart grow fonder. We stay apart and do our own things so we don't get on each other's nerves very much and we don't have such high expectations. But we know the partner is always still there to go back to eventually, and that we can expect to resume being a couple again for short periods in the future. Also airfares are always per person, so there's a considerable saving not having to pay them for my partner. The disadvantages to this setup are that some of the time I have to do all my own shopping and cooking, and occasionally I feel a bit lonely. There is a huge barrier of language and culture. I don't have a soulmate, and we can't talk together in any depth because we don't have enough language in common.

The advantages of married life taking place in a foreign country with a foreign wife are quite considerable because I'm recognised as being a foreigner out of my home comfort zone, so my wife tries to compensate by finding other mixed couples in the supermarket or out in public and introducing herself as a foreign wife, and then introducing me to the expatriate so we end up chatting, which is something I would never dare to do on my own. Sometimes the wife will invite these new-found couples home for tea and we get to know each other. I really could not do this sort of thing on my own. Our expectations of each other are reduced because of very obvious language and cultural differences, so my general social relationship shortcomings are masked by these differences. They would stand out as much more obvious if we were from the same country and culture.

The disadvantages of married life taking place in a foreign country with a foreign wife are that we can't understand each other half the time, and we're forced to reduce our dialogue to fairly basic conversation. Consequently we both lack having a soulmate to discuss and share deep topics with. On the other hand I get three meals a day put in front of me and a house to live in and I've got jobs to do around the house and garden, so there's a satisfaction element in these responsibilities.

So my foreign wife does provide some support to me finding expat-local couples, cooking three meals a day for me (but I usually end up eating them alone), providing free accommodation in her bungalow (but this is instead of paying interest on the large sums of money I've rather naïvely lent her). Sadly, though, she can't read in English so can't learn what AS is all about or understand my issues except in the simplest terms. She can't join forums or share any difficulties she has with me with other AS partnered wives and generally leaves me alone to solve my own problems.

If I had my time over again, I'm not sure what I would do differently in terms of relationships. I'm a bit cautious.

I think that has been wise in my case. I've had a pretty good life on the whole and learned to cope, so I don't think I'd want to change it vastly. I was very naïve and inexperienced as a teenager, so perhaps I'd be more careful about what I was letting myself in for. I think plunging into unknown areas in relationships can be a bit dangerous. But then 'nothing ventured nothing gained'.

Soon after my late diagnosis, which didn't come until I was well into my retirement years, I realised how much I'd been missing out on relationships and love life. I decided to try and correct this before it was too late. It made me realise that I'd been far too reserved and careful in such matters all my life. I crossed seas to a far away country and entered into a romance which lasted a month or two with another Aspie. There were a lot of problems. We were both Aspie but both on different sides of the spectrum, although we had a lot of things in common. However, there were a lot of bad things too and we ended up breaking up because of this, but my late diagnosis changed my whole attitude towards confidence in myself and I went out and did it, and I'm glad I did, even though it did end in failure. I don't know what happened to this lover in question. I got myself thrown out in the end. It was quite painful at the time but it was a big life experience.

The advice I would give to others with Asperger syndrome is not to fall prey to peer pressure to conform and follow like sheep do. Follow your passionate interests, but keep a bird's eye view of where you're heading.

Chapter 8

Meeting the Train

Alyssa Aleksanian

Introduction by Luke Beardon

Alyssa always seems to write from the heart – and, in reading what she has to say, it is clear why! Her 'no nonsense' approach is a superb indictment of what she stands for, and how her mind works. In this chapter Alyssa gives the reader a brilliant insight into what Asperger syndrome (AS) means to her, and the impact it has on her. The effort she has to make in her 'acting' roles comes across with great clarity, as does the conflict that can arise when effective communication is lacking. Her metaphors and stories are apt and poignant; she is superb at making her points with meaning and rationale – there is so much to learn about autism from reading this chapter, as well as it being a wonderful piece of writing in its own right.

Communication is the Big Deal for anyone with AS. It's the Gordian knot of Aspie issues. We've asked ourselves the following questions so many times, we've lost count: *Why did I get that reaction? What did I say wrong? How on earth did that disagreement begin?*

We strive to be precise with language as being misunderstood is an acutely painful experience. Perhaps it is this striving for clarity of speech makes us Aspies sound blunt...

I know that on a good day I can walk the neurotypical (NT) walk, I can talk the NT talk. On these NT days, my energy is high; I've had plenty of sleep, I have meditated and exercised. I have eaten well. I've spent time alone drawing and painting (i.e. used my special interests to recharge).

These are the days when, if I were to disclose my diagnosis of Aspergers, others would say: *Oh, you must have a very mild case* or *Really? But you're so calm and steady!*

That is because I'm a great observer. I've learnt 'the act'.

Adults with AS have had many years to absorb other people's mannerisms; how they interact and respond. It is a practised and rehearsed act. We know what it 'looks' like to fit in. We imitate.

But it takes enormous energy. These rehearsed responses are not innate. Formulating a response while in a social situation becomes a pure analytical and intellectual exercise.

For instance, if someone asks me a simple question, the following is a typical example of my thought process:

- I try to interpret the question: Am I hearing them right? What exactly do they mean?

- I see my own response clearly in my head as a picture.

- I scramble to translate that picture into words.

- I rehearse my verbal response silently and ask myself: Would that sound acceptable/sensible if I said it out loud?

- I think about the tone of voice I need to deliver the line.

- I adjust my stance or posture to mirror the other person.

- I make a mental note to glance at their face.

- I say the response out loud.

- I wait.

All of this happens in a few moments. It is not automatic. This script needs to be remembered. It is draining and it's taken years to perfect.

On a good day, I can remember the steps of this script in order. On a not-so-good day, the steps get muddled up or I forget an entire step (e.g. I forget to look at the person's face; my tone is monotonous; I misinterpret the question; etc.) and the result is a conversation faux pas.

By ourselves or relaxed with someone we trust, we Aspies don't need to follow a formulated step-by-step charade so closely. People who know us and love us make allowances. We may say the nonsensical thing, or act in the inappropriate way. But it's OK to become that little bit visible.

One cannot describe how glorious and precious a gift it is to be able to relax, express yourself and be accepted just as you are.

Then there are other days – the very Aspie days – when the energy to interact does not exist, there is no memory of the script and we can't go into the peopled world. Those are the days that we don't let others see. We withdraw. On these days aloneness is essential: it is as a need for air. The onslaught of the world is too loud, too chaotic and too bright. Those are the days of solitude. Then we become invisible on our own terms.

Communication in an Aspie's world is an unpredictable animal; it slips and moves. To our mind, our lack of control over it, the confusion and chaos inherent within it, is often the core reason to avoid it entirely.

Look me in the eye

Experts in the field say that people with AS miss facial cues. I hold the converse view. I say we don't miss anything. We pick up on *everything*.

Many Aspies can find it very disconcerting, even distressing, to look directly at someone when they talk. It's as though there's too much static or interference coming from the other's face – they literally become difficult to hear. Why? Because we pick up every twitch, every blink of an eye and every subtle movement of a line or a wrinkle: *There is too much information.*

I believe somewhere deep in our psyche, for the sake of our sanity, we chose not to look directly at people when they talk because facial expressions and body language hold too much, and often (most importantly), *contradict what the other is saying.*

For me, to watch someone's face as they talk, is like seeing the world through the long lens of a camera, zooming incessantly in and out. One's head starts feel fuzzy and things around and within start to slide. Nausea is the usual result. Try telling a friend: *'Looking at you makes me feel sick...'.*

The only way to stop the discomfort once it starts is to go to a quiet place and shut the metaphorical door.

Mean what you say

The subtle conversational dance that happens between NTs – the implied things, the tactful truths – people with Aspergers don't have this mechanism. It is a world we don't have access to; we can't seem to figure out the rules of that game.

We don't do casual. Our focus is 'hyperfocus' or not at all. As an Aspie friend once said:

I don't say anything more or less than what I mean... and what I say must be as much as possible, precise.

Our bluntness, our occasional inappropriateness tends to stem from our respect and, often times, compulsion for the truth. *We do not do subtext, play emotional games or intend to deceive.* Some of us are not capable of it; those of us who are, value honesty above all else and would not deceive on the strongest principle.

Precise, hard-won communication is too precious, rare and sometimes so frustrating for us to produce, how could we risk subverting it with innuendo?

There was a moment in a relationship, just after *another* misunderstanding, a boyfriend asked if I wanted to continue on with the relationship: *'Did I want to try to learn how to talk with one another?'* he asked. It was a very difficult question to answer.

After some considerable thought, I answered it with a metaphor: a one-sided, completely from my-own-Aspie-point-of-view kind of metaphor.

Communication, I concluded, is like a rail line. Communicating with someone is like standing between the rails, on those tracks. The train is the oncoming potential (and often inevitable) misunderstanding.

So what he was asking me, in essence, was a ridiculous question: Did I want to remain on the train tracks and wait for the train to run me over, then try and figure out what the misunderstanding was all about (while putting my emotional body parts back together)? Or, did I want to step off the tracks and walk away into the sunset; realising that being alone, although sometimes acutely lonely, was easier and far less painful than trying and failing to make a stable connection?

Given those two options, the decision seemed a no-brainer.

Yet, despite the hundreds, thousands, of times I have been at a loss to work out where the line of communication went awry, there I find myself again, standing on the tracks, waiting for the train.

So the question then becomes: Why do we Aspies do this to ourselves?

Possibly because I, like many with AS, can't believe in a world where we cannot make one authentic connection with another human being. To get off those tracks means we've lost all faith in our ability to find a true, genuine relationship. And frankly, to give up on that Holy Grail is a world many of us wouldn't want to live in.

Contrary to some 'professionals' opinion, we, with AS do long for human connection; we are just not very good at it.

There is a story about a Sufi mystic, Shams of Tabriz, that comes to mind here.

Shams was wandering the deserts of Persia for years, looking for a true friend, one that could really understand him. God's voice boomed down from the heavens and said:

'What would you give, Shams of Tabriz, for this one true friend?'

Shams, without hesitation, says, *'My head.'*

He, without flinching, would give his *all.*

It is after this encounter he finds Rumi, who later becomes the revered Sufi poet. Together Rumi and Shams spent hours in mystical conversation, lost in each other's company. A secret and special world of their own making.

This story strikes a deep chord with me. When I'm collecting my metaphorical body parts off the track, I remember this story. *Don't give up.*

This absolute friendship is what many Aspies long for.

'Do you come with instructions?'

Relationships can be bewildering for someone with Aspergers for a number of reasons.

- We have difficulty with the subtle social signals. Flirting can appear similar to other types of interactions. Being socially inexperienced, we may not pick up on the fact you're flirting with us and we won't know how to respond. Once, I laughed at a guy who tried to tell me quietly that he liked me. His voice had sounded odd and he was making a face I hadn't seen before. I didn't realise what he was implying and had no idea how to respond.

- We don't tend to have a group of friends who can vet our dates for us. Women in groups often talk about the men in their lives – what they did, what they said, how they said it. Most Aspies don't have a group of friends to help talk over prospective dates. As a consequence, we tend to go into relationships blind, believing what our new partner says, wanting to believe that he has our best interests at heart.

- We rely on the talk: We can mistrust ourselves to interpret another's actions correctly so instead, we rely on what someone says, often to the extent we ignore their dishonourable actions. We will believe someone who can 'talk us around', without realising that is what they are doing. We are incredibly loyal, so we often can't fathom that others are not.

- From what I can gather, a lot of communication within intimate relationships seems to be a complex dance of subtlety and innuendo; things unsaid but felt, and an awful lot implied. This is nightmare territory for someone with AS. We don't come with an NT's social dictionary, so an immense amount is lost in our attempt at internal translation. Remember that we are hypersensitive; emotions are felt intensely on the best of days. In a relationship where our feelings for the other person are amplified, add to this mix a confusion of unsaid but implied expectations and things we are supposed to 'get' without being told.

All of this means misunderstandings inevitably occur and things can start to come apart at the seams.

Inconsistency, broken promises and being unreliable are issues for any relationship, but for someone with AS they can be decisive deal breakers. It is not an exaggeration to say when those types of upsets occur, the metaphorical floor, walls and roof give way and there is terminal velocity into blackness for the relationship and the individual.

It would be fabulous if there was an instruction manual for relationships:

Chapter 1 What to say in certain emotionally charged situations

Chapter 2 What to do when you feel something amiss

Chapter 3 How to react when a once-steady bridge seems to be burning

But, of course, there is no such manual. People are individuals and everyone's instructions are different. As I have said, in everyday dealings, honesty is all important to an Aspie. But this element becomes the crucial key in a close relationship. If partners could say exactly what they mean and mean exactly what they say, a lot of Aspie relationship angst could be avoided. Clear, concrete statements are vital. A lot of our badgering and asking the same question over and over again is simply because we are trying to clarify; trying to figure out what something or someone means. We would much rather hear a comment harshly put than a vague statement where too much is implied. In 'subtly' there is too much to trip us up.

Chapter 9

Learning from Failed Relationships and Overcoming Sexual Obsession

David Walsh

Introduction by Luke Beardon

While at times this may make for uncomfortable reading, David has some excellent insights into his own Asperger syndrome (AS) and how it has impacted on his relationships. He is an advocate of early diagnosis, and demonstrates how an earlier diagnosis might have made a considerable difference to his understanding of self, and how this in turn may have influenced his relationships.

I face the prospect of writing about my intimate, sexual relationships with some trepidation. You see this is the area of my life that I associate with feelings of guilt and shame, and a sense of repeated failure. Even today, I do not know how to be successful in a long-term, intimate relationship with a woman. I suspect that I am not alone in this. I have learned something from over 30 years of experience of trying to develop lasting, intimate relationships and it is this that I would like to share with you.

I shall start with a brief account of some of my experiences of sexual and intimate relationships. I will then reflect on how I could have made them more successful, positive experiences with the benefit of what I now know.

As a boy, I was a shy loner who was afraid of many things. I had a particular hang up about urinating at school. I demonstrated considerable willpower and control to be able to last all day without urinating. Unfortunately, I perverted this difficulty into a fetish around a natural bodily function that rapidly became an overwhelming long-term sexual obsession. I recall powerful feelings of excitement around this fetish, even as a young boy. I also felt shame and disgust. It is difficult for me to write about this, but I think it is important that I do, as these early childhood thoughts and experiences had a profound negative impact on my subsequent attempts at intimate and sexual relationships. I should add that I am aware that many people feel that their unusual sexual practices are fine as long as they do not hurt other people. I will return to this subject later.

My first real sexual experience was at college. I met a woman at a dance class and we dated a few times. I was frustrated by how little she spoke, even though it was clear that she was highly intelligent. I cannot recall quite how I found myself one evening lying on her bed stroking her breasts for four hours. I do remember feeling troubled by the fact that this was not arousing me. I left her flat with a dejected feeling, immediately after staunching a nosebleed. This depressing incident merely served to deepen my depressed state of mind and lack of self-worth.

I had to wait five years for my next sexual encounter. I was working in Holland and I had befriended a Dutch woman in an Irish bar. She seemed to enjoy my humour. She was very attractive to my eyes. Having established that she might be interested in me, I invited her for a meal at my house. I recall extreme fear at being alone with such an attractive young woman, and much confusion about what I was feeling. At one point she undressed and lay corpse-like on the bed. This is the moment that filled me with terror. I tried to delay the start of any physical contact by bizarrely suggesting that we watch an episode of my favourite sitcom at the time, *Cheers*. I think I had in mind the arousal difficulty at college. The evening ended quickly with me taking the woman home. Yet again I felt worthless and very depressed about my failure to perform sexually. I do recall this Dutch woman commenting on why I never seemed to want to see her that often.

In my late 20s, I tried to meet women through social clubs and dating agencies. I started dating a married woman who was separated from her husband. I realise now that she was struggling to come to terms with this situation. She had difficulties with sexual arousal, and I was probably the worst possible kind of person for her to get involved with. At the time, I did not understand the meaning of empathy, and I clearly was not in a position to give her the emotional support she so badly needed. I hated myself for always seeming to focus on some less attractive feature of her body, whilst at the same time obsessing on her beautiful blue eyes. The stress of the relationship reached breaking point after six weeks and, after a day of silence, I decided to walk out of her house. She chased me up the street and hit me in the nose. This time I did not get a nosebleed! I must have been the source of such confusion and frustration for this unhappy woman.

I finally lost my virginity at the age of 29. I had answered an ad in a singles magazine. Kate (not her real name) was an extraordinary young woman. She had a serious health problem involving her heart that limited what she could do physically, but she had a lust for life and I was instantly attracted to her. I have fond memories of intense conversations in the first few weeks as we got to know each other. She helped me overcome some of my fear of sexual intimacy, but all the problems that had affected my earlier attempts at close relationships soon came to the fore. I started obsessing about physical imperfections again. Kate was highly sexed and I found this stressful. I found it difficult to sleep. I was filled with many negative emotions as I struggled to understand my true feelings for Kate. I found it difficult to talk about what I was thinking and feeling, and instead I focused on the area where I felt most confident – rational and intellectual discussion, probably communicated with a slightly superior manner. I think this made Kate feel inadequate though I was probably not aware of this at the time. I ended the relationship after two months. I remember being confused by the powerful emotions that Kate expressed towards the end of the relationship. I felt guilt and sadness, but the desire to be on my own seemed more appealing than the stress of being in this unhealthy, co-dependent relationship. Painful as it is to confess to this now, incorporating my fetish into our sexual activities also had a profoundly negative influence on our relationship, although it was also a source of excitement.

I think that this is enough on my past intimate and sexual relationships, suffice as to note that I will always be eternally grateful to one woman who gave me the feedback I badly needed that led me to seek professional help and eventually to get a diagnosis of Asperger syndrome (AS). The last four years have been an amazing time for me, a time of learning and self-discovery. I still live alone, but I feel more confident and I suffer less from depression. I have a few good friends and I do not feel so alone. This is a good time to reflect on my failed relationships and perhaps to offer helpful advice to young Aspies who might acknowledge some similar experiences to those I have had.

I see now that one of the reasons why I continued to fail in attempts at close relationships was my lack of self-awareness. I assumed that I was normal and that I should be able to do all the things that other people do. I incorrectly attributed failure in relationships to the fact that I must be ugly, bad or not masculine enough. Anthony Robbins calls this making false neuro-associations.[1] If I had had an early diagnosis of AS, and learned how this might impact my social interactions through a lack of emotional awareness and empathy, I think I would have been more able to see the true cause of a failed attempt at developing an intimate relationship. It was not that I was ugly or bad, but rather that I lacked adequate emotional and social skills.

I wish I had the answers to how to successfully develop emotional awareness and empathy, but I do not. I believe that these are some of the key areas that put Aspies at such a disadvantage when it comes to achieving successful, intimate relationships. I have tried a number of activities to develop emotional and social skills, but I suspect that for maximum impact they need to be done at the earliest appropriate age, and not in your 40s. I have read that the brain continues to develop up to the age of about 19. This is why I am a strong advocate of early diagnosis, so any subsequent educational programme to develop emotional and social skills has the best chance of success. The kinds of activities that I mean are to be found in references such as that written by Judith Martinovich.[2] I can recommend the Mind Reading software developed at the University of Cambridge for helping to better interpret emotions from facial expressions.[3]

I realise now that low self-esteem and confidence contributed to a defeatist attitude in my attempts to meet women for a relationship, and the fetish exacerbated this. I think it is really important to do things that develop and

1   Robbins, A. (2001) *Awaken the Giant Within: How to Take Immediate Control of Your Mental, Emotional, Physical and Financial Life.* London: Simon & Schuster.

2   Martinovich, J. (2006) *Creative Expressive Activities and Asperger's Syndrome: Social and Emotional Skills and Positive Life Goals for Adolescents and Young Adults.* London: Jessica Kingsley Publishers.

3   Baron-Cohen, S. (2007) *Mind Reading: The Interactive Guide to Emotions 1.3.* London: Jessica Kingsley Publishers. See www.jkp.com/mindreading

maintain high self-esteem. I do a number of things that help with this. I use affirmations. I do some voluntary work. I give to various charities. I think of all the good things that have happened in the day before I go to sleep. I try to exercise regularly. I socialise more. I try not to be so hard on myself when I occasionally relapse with my sexual obsession.

I suspect I have done most of my learning of social skills through trial and error in my day-to-day social interactions with friends and colleagues at work. I think I would have learned more quickly if I had had more supportive feedback from people able to tell me how I could improve my communication in specific situations. I think there should be more opportunities for Aspies like me to test new ways of interacting in a supportive environment through role playing. I think this should be a core part of school education. I think neurotypical (NT) children would also benefit.

I think I should give some feedback on my extensive experience of using dating services. My experiences have mostly been negative. I paid £1000 to join one dating agency, only to discover weeks later that it had gone bankrupt. I never saw my £1000 again. Dating and singles organisations are designed to meet the needs of NT people. They assume a level of confidence and emotional awareness. I think there is a need for more specialist dating services for AS people. I do not want to suggest that AS adults should not try dating services, though I see particular risks using such services as speed dating.

I think AS people can learn to be better at reading the non-verbal language of attraction and flirting. I have often missed these cues, causing frustration and irritation in the other person. I suggest reading books on the subject, such as that written by Allan and Barbara Pease.[4] Parents and friends can help by encouraging the Aspie to notice such body language in people around them. I am certainly more

---

4   Pease, A. and Pease, B. (2004) *The Definitive Book of Body Language*. London: Orion Books.

able now to spot gestures that might indicate attraction, such as the movement of a hand through hair.

I have learned that you cannot and should not act or fake an emotional connection with someone. I think the stress that I experienced in my early relationships might have been partly caused by an unconscious attempt to try to emulate the observed behaviour of others in relationships. I think you have to be true to yourself even if this means acknowledging a difficulty with emotional reciprocity.

I understand now that obsessing on one part of the body rather than seeing a person holistically is a common AS trait. I think it is important to help AS people who want to start dating realise that this might happen, and the negative effect of this on any relationship.

I needed help to deal with my sexual obsession. I was fortunate to find a specialist counsellor who introduced me to Dr Patrick Carnes's programme for sexual addicts, based on the Twelve Steps of Alcoholics Anonymous.[5] I have worked through this programme and it has helped me feel more empowered to handle my sexual obsession. Steps 8 and 9 require that you list all people you have harmed, and then make direct amends to these people. I felt the strong need to make amends to Kate, so I made contact after six years. We met and she listened to what I needed to say and I was able to make amends. Eight months later I heard that she had died at the age of 42 from a complication related to her faulty heart.

With the benefit of hindsight I think an observant person might have been able to identify behaviour related to my sexual obsession at an early age. I would urge any parent or carer to look for early signs of behaviour that might indicate development of an unhealthy obsession with sex. The easy access to pornography on the internet is not helpful. I did not feel able to talk about my fetish with anyone, because I

---

5   Carnes, P. (2001) *Facing the Shadow: Starting Sexual and Relationship Recovery.* Carefree, AZ: Gentle Path Press.

was so ashamed. Instead I kept that part of my life secret. I think that it is so important to feel able to talk about inappropriate sexual behaviour rather than let it negatively affect self-esteem and perhaps lead to depression. I have felt quite ashamed about my inappropriate sexual behaviour. I am aware that it risks debasing women by considering them as little more than objects. I do try to control this sexual obsession by going to extreme measures such as setting parental control on my computer and storing the administrator's password at work. Isabelle Hénault discusses inappropriate sexual behaviour such as fetishes in her book about Asperger syndrome and sexuality.[6] In my life I have given up smoking and managed to overcome a 20-year habit of alcohol abuse. I can tell you that controlling my sexual addiction has been much more of a challenge than either the smoking or the drinking. I have written at length on this subject, because I think it is a particular risk for young adults with AS, with their lack of empathy, and I believe it can lead to mental health problems and a major barrier to the achievement of happiness through successful intimate relationships. I see evidence for this from messages on AS discussion forums.

I find analogy helpful in trying to understand how I might be different from NT people in the area of emotions and their role in relationships. Here is one example. I think of emotions as electrical currents. When I am with someone I do have a sense of my mood and emotional state. However, as soon as I am apart from this person, I have great difficulty recalling how I felt. I seem to have a poor ability to recall emotional memories. This means I can easily forget about important people in my life, such as close friends and family. In an electrical circuit, the capacitor has the ability to store electrical charge, which can be released later as required. You see its effect, for example, when you switch off

---

6   Hénault, I. (2006) *Asperger's Syndrome and Sexuality: From Adolescence through Adulthood*. London: Jessica Kingsley Publishers.

a computer powered from the mains through a transformer. The green light on the transformer stays lit for several seconds after disconnecting the plug. The capacitor stores electrical charge (the potential for an electrical current) as a normal limbic brain stores emotional memories. I think I (along with many AS people) must have a differently wired limbic brain that either does not store emotional memories, or cannot readily access them. I think analogy can sometimes be helpful in communicating complex ideas.

I have learned to accept that I cannot suddenly acquire emotional awareness and empathy. I have come to the conclusion that it is better for me to be open about any emotional difficulties with any woman that I meet where there may be a possible mutual attraction. I struggle to overcome the fear that surfaces when I find myself in the position where I should disclose something of my emotional difficulties. I know that I need to face this fear, but it would be so much easier if I could practise this scenario in a supportive environment through role play with constructive feedback and practice. I think AS people would greatly benefit from such specialist counselling and coaching.

I think it is important to try to develop friendships first, rather than focusing on sexual relationships. You can learn many useful social skills through interactions with friends that will help in the more intimate relationships later. I have found it less stressful learning in this way. I get a lot of personal enjoyment from intellectual chats with friends. There have been times when this has brought us together. Perhaps these have been the most intimate moments in my life to date.

I have learned the importance of social reciprocity. This seems even more important if it is difficult to offer emotional reciprocity. I use thinking strategies to mitigate my lack of emotional awareness. When a girlfriend rang me once to tell me she was ill, I did not feel anything but I did know that sending her a get well card and flowers was a good thing to do.

Finally, I would like to recommend Maxine Aston's helpful book, *Aspergers in Love*.[7] I learned a lot from reading this book, even though I have never been in a loving relationship. I particularly liked the chapter, 'Benefits of Asperger Syndrome', because it lists some of the benefits that an NT partner sees in their AS partner. I have found it helpful to write down the positive qualities that I have that might be beneficial in a relationship. I suggest this as a useful activity. Although I have not been successful at long-term intimate relationships, I have been successful at long-term friendships. I can now see that it is some of the qualities that I have from being an Aspie that have made me attractive to people who have become close friends, such as loyalty and trustworthiness, being a good listener, being witty with an intelligent and enthusiastic curiosity about life. I am beginning to see the kind of 'loving' relationship that might be within my ability to achieve by applying all that I have now learned. A part of me does question whether I even want an intimate, long-term relationship. It is the norm in society, but I seem to need to be alone more than most people, and brief but rewarding activities with good friends do seem to satisfy much of my need to be with other people. The one area that is not satisfied is the need for sexual satisfaction.

I am optimistic that the next generation of Aspies can learn faster than I have learned about what it takes to have a successful long-term relationship. However, this will require effective, innovative educational programmes that aim to develop emotional and social skills from an early age.

---

7   Aston, M. (2003) *Aspergers in Love: Couple Relationships and Family Affairs.* London: Jessica Kingsley Publishers.

Chapter 10

The Infatuation That Almost Killed Me

Anthony Sclafani

Introduction by Luke Beardon

Anthony's chapter elucidates so well just how much of an impact an individual can have on a person on the spectrum – often, without that person even knowing about it. I think it must be pretty difficult for anyone who has not gone through the kind of emotional extremes that Anthony has done to appreciate just how powerful those emotions can be, but in this chapter Anthony eloquently describes his experiences and the influence they have had on him. It has been reported by some people with autism that rather than being emotionally bereft (which is occasionally how people with autism are viewed) they feel emotions to extreme levels; this certainly appears to be the case with Anthony. What comes through in this chapter, aside from the obvious impact on Anthony, is the apparent lack of support available for a person who is going through such a difficult time. It is crucial that those working in the autism field have a good understanding of the experiences of people like Anthony in order to be able to support them in an appropriate way – and Anthony's chapter does a fantastic job of providing a narrative of just how important that support could be.

I am a 39-year-old male from New York City with Asperger syndrome (AS). I was diagnosed with it back in 2001 after having symptoms of it for most of my life. I currently have a full-time job in a Registrar's Office at a Community College. I never had any romantic experience with a woman before. I am straight but I am an inexperienced virgin. Due to my AS it is difficult for me to make friends and especially to develop relationships. I never had that many friends and I was never good with dealing with my peer group. There are times that physical contact is also difficult for me. I am ticklish and am sensitive to being touched. I do not freak out when I get touched but it seems I feel it more than other people. These weaknesses do bother me but at this age I have somewhat accepted them. I would like to meet someone of the opposite sex one of these days, but it's not easy.

In this chapter I am going to discuss a specific event in my life that affected me greatly. The event is when I had an infatuation with a woman. This happened when I was a student in college.

This event takes place back in the fall of 1996. It was the first day of classes at my college. This was the college that I studied in, not the one I work for now. I was sitting in my first class of the day. It was a sociology course which started early in the morning. While I was sitting listening to the professor's lecture a woman sat at the desk next to me. For some reason I did not like this woman even though I never saw or met her before. To this day I could never explain why. The class goes on and then it ends. As I get ready to pack up to leave the classroom the woman turns to me and asks me where is the library? I explained to her where it was and all of the sudden we started talking to each other. I introduced myself to her and she introduced herself. For some reason I kind of opened up to her, of course I never mentioned my prior mysterious dislike towards her. I offered to walk her to the library and she accepted. As we walk towards the library we continue to discuss about ourselves. We then talked about our prior schooling. For some reason I mentioned that I was in Special Ed and had some problems, I did not know anything about AS back then. She mentioned a little about herself including that she went to a Gifted school most of her life. She had some challenges too but mostly they were different than mine. It appeared that even though we were different we had a similar wavelength in conversation. I felt comfortable talking to her and she seemed to get along with me pretty well. She then goes to the library and I go on my way. As the day passed I thought quite a bit about this encounter. I felt good, confident and eager to see her again.

I did see her again and spoke to her again, many times. As I continued talking to her I discovered that the sociology course was the only course we had together. I find out that we had the same 70-minute break in between the sociology course and the next course. I took advantage of this break to see and speak to her. I find out she is living with her boyfriend in a nearby apartment. The boyfriend is eight years older than her and he's a bodybuilder. She transferred from two other previous colleges. The first college she did not like plus she had an abusive prior boyfriend there that she had to put a restraining order on. The second college ended up not working out because she was not interested in the majors there. I then find out that this college, the third one, was temporary because she was trying to get into another college, a better one. She applied to that other college so many times over the years but for some reason they would not accept her.

She mentioned her mother and stepfather lived out of state and she would occasionally visit them every other weekend. We both had no siblings. We had the same major, psychology. As the semester went on I became very obsessed with her. I became depressed and melancholy. I started to analyse myself a lot and started comparing myself to other people my age. I also started to imagine myself being involved with her. I was in a very odd way during this time. I had to see her and talk to her during that break but crazy enough when I saw her outside of this break and the sociology course I felt shy and funny seeing her. For a while I thought she knew something was up. I would even inquire, 'Am I getting too close?' She indicated no and that she had a number of male platonic friends and preferred them to female friends at times. Based on the situation I never wanted her (even to this day) to know how I really felt about her and what I was going through. It would just cause too many problems that I did not need or could handle. During this time I was getting funny feelings. I called them the 'waves'. I do not know if it was anxiety based or if I was really in love. Every time I would think of her or see a relationship on TV I would get these feelings. After a while I could not watch certain TV shows anymore due to these 'waves'.

Registration then comes for the next semester, spring 1997. We both liked the professor of the sociology course so we both tried to get into it. I was able to get into it because I had an earlier registration appointment as I was part of the Students with Disabilities programme back then. She tried to register during her registration appointment but was not successful. She tried to get an overtally for the course but the Sociology Department declined. I tried to get into a few of the courses she was registered for but that did not work and I did not want to appear to be stalking her. I was also not too interested in the courses she ended up registering for anyway. At first I was crushed when she did not get into the sociology course with me for the spring but we discovered that we both had an early morning course at the same time, which included a brief break in between that course and the next one. It was only a 20-minute break but it was something, I guess.

A short time after spring registration the final exam period starts for the fall semester. This is a pretty stressful time because of the final exams. We both decide to get together to study for the sociology final. She offered to let me to go to her apartment to study. I declined because of her boyfriend and I felt funny going up to a stranger's apartment, even though she was not really a stranger. I did not tell her this directly but I think she picked up my feelings about the offer. She indicated her boyfriend was not the jealous or suspicious type. We ended up agreeing to meet in the library to study. We did get together a few times to study in the library for the upcoming final. There were a few times she called me at home regarding the course. This was cool since we stayed on the phone a while and talked about other things. We did talk about the course material also. The day of the final came. Right before the test she mentioned that she wanted to get together to meet during the intercession break and said that she would call me. I absolutely accepted. We did not make any specific plans there since it was the final exam period and the Christmas holiday was right around the corner. The finals came and went. I did pretty good grades that semester despite what I was going through.

The intercession break lasted a little over a month. I waited desperately to hear from her. I did not have the guts or courage to call her directly about this, so I just waited around. Throughout that time I just kept thinking about her, getting her call and the whole experience I went through. I was in pretty bad shape. I even thought about ending it all but never attempted to do so, thank goodness. I just couldn't get over this. I did try talking to some of my friends and even a few family members about this but their advice did not really help me that much.

The spring semester starts and I go to my first class. After the class ended I go outside, where we always would hang out last semester, to see if she was there. Sure enough she was there. We spoke about the holidays a little. She did apologise for not calling me during the intercession. It was good seeing her again. For the next few weeks I would see her during that brief break. Even though I was glad to see and talk to her I still was not well. I was still going through the same feelings and thoughts that I had last semester.

Then there were a couple of times that I did not see her. In the back of my head I would question if she was probably avoiding me for some reason. Then I saw her again and she indicated that some things came up. During this time I pushed myself to become friendlier with other fellow students. This worked to some extent and did make me feel better but the reality was that I was still suffering with being infatuated with her. During these attempts I think I was subconsciously trying to meet another woman similar to her and hoping for better success.

Into the midpoint of the semester she did not show up a number of times. I was becoming concerned since this was for a longer period of time than previously. Then one day I finally see her. She's really sad, she tells me her grandfather died. She was very close to her grandfather because she did not have a father figure when she was growing up. Her parents divorced when she was very young. I felt really bad and hugged her. I don't think she liked me hugging her in that sudden fashion but it was brief and she did not say anything about it. We did talk about the death a bit and I tried offering some assistance. She appreciated my support.

A couple of weeks later I find out that she was accepted to the college that she was trying to get into. She is so happy. I find out that she will start classes next semester and this semester will be her last. When I heard this I congratulated her and was able to hold back my feelings about this, which was amazing for me. I was real crushed; I was not going to see her again. I really did not know what to do.

The end of the semester then comes. It was really hard for me to study for my finals between being infatuated with her and with her leaving. There was some good news though. All of our finals were on the same day so we were able to meet in between our tests. We spent a lot of time together that day. I treated her to lunch; we studied together (even though we were not in the same courses together), walked around outside and talked. She gave me her e-mail address. I did take it but back in 1997 I did not have a computer with internet access, did not have any e-mail address and had never even been on the internet before. I had her phone number but was not going to call her because of my discomfort with her live-in boyfriend, I just did not feel right calling her out of the blue. We did decide to write letters to each other. I did give her my address and I got her address. Right before the last test I walked her to the last exam. She asked if she could hug me, I said yes. We hugged each other. She stated that I was a real nice guy and it was a pleasure meeting me. We reminded each other to keep in touch. She then went to her exam and I went to my exam.

That summer was a rough one for me. All I kept thinking about was her and what I went through. I really did not want to do anything in regards to taking another course during the summer or taking another job. I was already doing part-time work in the college that I work for now but that was only on a short term basis during the busier part of their registration period. One of my counsellors at my college tried to help me get through this. I would see her once or twice a week about this. The counsellor would assign me to write about all of my feelings in regards to this experience. We would then discuss what I wrote and I would write more things. It was not easy. The counsellor did try but my problems weren't really solved. I did get a letter from her talking about her summer, etc. This made me feel good because she was keeping in touch. I did write back.

When the fall semester started I did still see the counsellor in regard to this, not as much though. As the semester progresses I get a call at my house. It's her, I am so happy. We talked that evening on the phone forever. We talked about the courses we were taking and all sorts of things going on. A few months later I get another letter from her. I wrote her again. For a while I did not hear from her. I was still in a shaky way at that point but it appeared that I was moving on a bit. The 'waves' were not as bad. A long while later I get another letter from her. This was the last letter that I would receive from her. In the letter she was stating that she was moving to California to become an occupational therapist. She got into a very good college there and was interested in the field of occupational therapy. I wrote her another letter and asked her for her new address. She never replied to that letter.

A few years later I get a computer with internet access. At this point (2001/2002) I was more comfortable with using the internet. Even though I was almost over the infatuation experience I wanted to e-mail her since I still had her e-mail address. She never replied to the e-mail. I discovered that her e-mail was AOL based. I had AOL messenger by then since I talked to my online buddies on it. I tried contacting her through that. I was successful. We did talk a few times on it but eventually it did not work out. She was hardly online because she was busy with her studies and the computer she had was really slow. Every time we would talk on there her computer would slow down and freeze. Whether this was true or not was another story.

A number of years later, actually around two years ago, I found her on Facebook. For a while I had hesitation contacting her through there since it was so long ago but I figure what the hell I would try anyway. She remembered me and accepted my friend request on Facebook. She now lives in Florida and is now a busy occupational therapist who also is into boxing and keeping herself fit. She seems different now and she knows more people. We have spoken on there a few times at length but things are different now. She did come back to New York City a few times but we never met or made specific arrangements to do so. At this point I'm not inclined to see her. It has been so long and I am almost completely over the infatuation and do not really want to open up old wounds. I noticed that when I see TV or movies from 1996 and 1997 the experience comes back to mind. The same thing goes when I hear a song from those two years. This might not seem to be a big deal now but this really took a toll on me for a number of years.

Chapter 11

A Relationship Is Not a Hobby

*It's a Full-Time Commitment,
Like It or Not!*

Norman Bridge

Introduction by Luke Beardon

Norman provides an excellent account of his experiences, and makes the notable point about whether a relationship is more likely to 'work' if the partner also has Asperger syndrome (AS) or, in his words, is AS-friendly. Compatibility is usually deemed to be a useful commodity for a successful relationship – but does this mean that two individuals with autism are more likely to get on than one with autism and one without? Without proper evidence this is not possible to answer – what is highly likely, though, is that a level of understanding and acceptance of who a person is, and how their autism impacts upon them, could be an essential component of a lasting relationship. Presumably, getting to know the various quirks of a partner and fully embracing them (or happily putting up with them) is a necessary aspect of any relationship; however, it may well be that the 'quirks' of a person with autism are perhaps more pronounced, or at odds with convention, than those of the predominant neurotype. If this is the case, then some level of empathic understanding would presumably be of huge benefit to the partner, in order to understand the nature of the quirks. This does not mean that the partner has to be on the spectrum, of course, nor does it mean that if the partner is on the spectrum it will mean they automatically have the empathy needed! Either way, embracing and enjoying the autism-related aspects of an individual's way of being seems to be a pretty good basis for a relationship.

I'm a single, unmarried and childless 40-something. I have had two romantic relationships in my life but for the most part I have been single. My feelings about this have been mixed. Growing up, it seemed the norm to be brought up by your biological parents who had been happily married for many years. The home life of myself, my friends and most of my relatives was just like that. I automatically assumed that the vast majority of people married in their 20s, and had children. I had no reason to think that I would be any different.

I know Aspies around their 50s and 60s who are or have been married, and have children, but it seems that it was once easier to meet partners, because communities tended to be more close knit. Nowadays people keep to themselves more and, if you went to an event at a pub, the social dynamics would be harder to negotiate and you might need to be fairly confident to get into a conversation with a decent person.

I never managed to make such an approach because I had to filter out all the noise and other distractions going on, never mind trying to figure out how I can approach them without getting it all wrong and making them feel uncomfortable. I believe that the discos that teenagers went to back in the 1960s were set up in such a way that it was expected that the boys would choose girls to ask for a dance, and nothing negative would ever be thought of it, whilst these days, it seems that perhaps the only event where you can be sure you wouldn't potentially cause offence just by talking to someone, would be a singles evening. At those there must be a bit of pressure because you do have to keep conversation flowing which is not the case when dancing.

Sometimes I'm jealous of grown men who are married with children. However, with some of the limitations that having Asperger syndrome can bring to my everyday life, then sometimes I feel less jealous of them, and can see just how much freedom I actually have, and indeed I cope better in life when I'm free rather than feeling constrained.

The advice here for males is not to wait for prospective partners to come to you as it rarely happens. That said, I did actually get asked out by three different women before finally agreeing to go out with one. The first girl was at school and one of the more pretty and popular girls. Like a fool, I turned her down for someone who wasn't interested. The other girl I turned down was much younger than me and extremely naïve; in hindsight she probably had mild learning difficulties or even AS.

Having people being romantically interested, as nice as it is, is pretty useless if you don't know how to actually do something about it. One woman, who I apparently shared a mutual attraction with, I did actually set about approaching on my last day at college in a corridor but this time the sudden appearance of a random passer-by ruined my plan. For years of college and university after that a similar pattern occurred, although usually the attraction wasn't mutual. If I had gone about things the right way then I'm fairly sure that I would have had more partners in my teens and 20s. It would not have even mattered if each relationship was short lived, as my first ever relationship in my late 20s was, because it would have been experience.

Even though straight after that first relationship it was back to being single again for a few years, I was actually able to refer to someone as my 'ex-girlfriend'. During that short time, it was great to finally experience that sort of bond with someone of the opposite sex and do couply things. One time whilst we were in town holding hands I heard one guy say to his friend 'Look at him strutting his stuff.' I must have been so over the moon to actually be able to do that, that I felt about ten feet tall. I think that if you have AS and as a result find it harder to meet people that you have to be open-minded and not too quick to dismiss potential partners unless there's a very good reason for a 'deal breaker'.

At about 30, for the first time in my life, I was in a serious relationship. This was with a fellow Aspie and lasted close to a year. In many ways our shared diagnosis and understanding of each other's Aspie ways helped. She was a bit like a female version of myself and we became soulmates and shared some wonderful times together doing things together and spending time together. She was a very special person and I will always look back on this time extremely fondly. However, ironically, whilst some of our Aspie ways brought us closer together, others clashed and made the relationship very challenging at times. Needless to say, relationships need to be worked on and I did everything in my power to keep us together but, ultimately, after looking for solutions, it became too stressful for us both. We almost reunited a year later but I will always cherish the time that we did have together and don't regret a single second.

Since then, I have been on a few dates with different women, one of which added up to several dates and almost a relationship. I think asking someone to become your partner is always going to be an awkward area. Some will expect to be asked and others might expect to go with the flow if you are already going out on dates together. Non-Aspies probably get it wrong sometimes and people with AS perhaps more so and maybe go about it more awkwardly but you can only do what seems right to you at the time and you can't knock yourself for trying. Most women will be happy that someone was interested, and if a polite attempt is rebuffed rudely, that really says far more about the rude person than about someone who can hold their head up high for being a nice person who just wants to make someone happy.

It eventually reached the point that online dating became too expensive to continue. I felt that I needed to work on myself before being ready to share my life with someone else. The ways in which I like to spend my free time may seem a bit too obscure to really want to share some of it with others. At the moment I feel that I need space to be quirky in my own way, and I've noticed how much I need and value my own space. By the time I've done a 37-hour working week, sorted out my evening meal and cleaned my flat, I'm already tired.

Added to that I have other responsibilities outside of work that aren't so easy to be liberated from but, even if I was, the chances are that I just wouldn't cope with so little time to myself unless a partner was willing to meet me on my terms with her only visiting me at certain times on week nights and us sticking to simple activities like making a meal together and watching TV. I could perhaps visit her at weekends and be more adventurous then but I'd need the chance to lie in on both days and take naps. How nice it would be to be with someone who only expected my company as often as I wanted hers.

I'm not sure how many partners would be so accepting of this. Not very many, I'd imagine. There would probably be more chance of finding a needle in a haystack. Girlfriends are not hobbies, they have feelings and need you to feel committed to them and in most cases will want to have contact with you more than once a day, unless it's a very casual relationship that is probably very new.

As for children, when I got to about 40, rather than beating myself up for still being single and childless, I suddenly came to the realisation that my need even for a partner to compromise on when to spend time with me means that fatherhood would be a life change that I simply would not be equipped to handle without some other significant lifestyle change, such as only working part time.

I still wouldn't rule marriage out but a wife would need to be very accepting of my need to spend lots of time alone and ideally not have nor want children. My age now will make the prospect of finding someone not wishing to have children in the future more likely since otherwise I'd almost certainly need to marry someone younger.

An Aspie partner may be more accepting as she might also need lots of alone time and be more understanding of a wide variety of Aspie quirks that a non-Aspie individual might not find normal. This of course does depend on the respective Aspie quirks not clashing too much and the couple being able to support each other.

I personally would be best suited to someone fairly placid like myself. The ex-girlfriend that wasn't Aspie (to my knowledge), I suspect of mild learning difficulties. The two girls from online dating that I got on with best both had some AS traits but perhaps not enough to get diagnosed. Either way they were certainly AS-friendly. Had a relationship taken place with either one, it would have been interesting to see if it would have survived when my mask slipped and the AS traits emerged. I did not disclose. It remains to be seen whether I can only survive a relationship with a fellow Aspie or if it would need to be with a non-Aspie to stand the test of time. I'd be very interested to see what it would be like in a relationship with someone not on the spectrum and if there are any that would be willing to accept my mild symptoms.

Life certainly has not turned out in the traditional way that I would have expected. A part of me feels selfish for not contributing to the continuation of mankind because if everyone copied me then the human race would die out. However, I realise now that to keep mankind going you have to genuinely care for a real live human being with feelings from birth to adulthood. As someone with AS it can be challenging enough to look after myself at times. I am a bit disappointed not to be bringing anyone into the world but some people are 'born' parents and others are not. Besides with the ever increasing population of the world, can it really hurt if a few people give parenting a miss?

I think I can travel quite contentedly towards 50 without having any children and not be too perturbed if I'm not married or engaged by then, I would prefer to have some form of romantic relationship again in the future. I would find it depressing if there is nothing at all, but for now I'm happy to just go with the flow and just hope that someone comes along one day. I'm happy just being me and enjoying each day as it comes. This year I might go on holiday alone, who knows where and just be free and happy to just be, and enjoy life just living in the moment.

Chapter 12

Accepting Each Other
(aka Chapter Twelve)[1]

Alexandra Brown

Introduction by Luke Beardon

Alex certainly writes in a refreshingly direct style, and provides some excellent insight into what a relationship means to her. She does not pretend to have all the answers, she simply writes about how she feels about relationships, what is important, and what is not. It is illuminating to read about how Alex recognises some of the characteristics of Asperger syndrome (AS) and what impact they might have on a relationship. Her views on romance, for example, are brilliantly articulated, though they may go against convention! When reading her views, however, they are persuasive in their logic, and it is easy to see why she holds the views she does.

Whilst I am certainly no expert on relationships, I can share some observations and conclusions I have reached over the years.

---

1   This is the fourth in the series of books that I have contributed to; my chapter in the first book was called 'Chapter Three' and in the second it was called 'Chapter Six'. In the third, the format changed, but to keep the sequence my chapter was the ninth and had '(aka Chapter Nine)' in the title. Hence the (aka) here!

First, here's a bit of background information. I have been with my husband David since February 1989 and we married in 1997. Our daughter was born in 1990. I have only had one other relationship prior to this, so I do not have much experience in terms of the number of relationships I have to draw upon, nor the range or variety (if there is such a thing), so it's more about how my own relationship has progressed, the things I have learned and what I have observed in others.

As a person with Asperger syndrome, I might consider myself an expert in the field of observation, as that is how I seem to spend a lot of my life outside the home, in particular in social situations. I am not interested in social media or what is going on in the celebrity world and, thankfully, I think they are a law unto themselves.

Some people say that opposites attract and some people think it helps to be very alike; I couldn't really comment on whether either is right, however, there are some criteria I believe to be important in a successful relationship:

- friendship

- sense of humour

- respect

- trust

- similar values.

I think that friendship is important, whether it comes before the start of a relationship or it evolves as a part of the relationship. You are likely to be spending a lot of time together and you need a strong base to build your relationship on.

It helps if you have a similar sense of humour, or at least understand your partner's sense of humour. Some people think that individuals with Asperger syndrome don't have a sense of humour, but I believe it is just a case of it being different to theirs or, alternatively, if you are in a stressful situation, you're hardly likely to be in a position to be able to understand or demonstrate humour, you tend to go into survival mode. Humour can sustain you through some of the more difficult times, even where it is only seeing the irony in a situation.

Mutual respect is a key component to any relationship, along with trusting your partner. It is difficult to build a strong relationship without trust, however, the person you are placing your trust in should be worthy of it. How you tell that, though, is another matter. I think the same could also be said of a friendship, however, you are likely to be investing more of yourself emotionally into a personal relationship and therefore you will want to get it right. In general, I like to see the good in people and at one point would have had no reason to doubt putting my trust or faith in someone, but experience teaches you that not everyone is like that, and the world isn't like that. I know in the past I would probably not have listened to other people, I would not have liked them questioning my judgement, or may have been suspicious of their motives, but if you happen to have someone you trust and they are telling you there are issues, or they have concerns about the person you are with, then it is probably at least worth listening to what they have to say and considering their point of view.

We all have a system of values, of beliefs by which we live our lives. As I was growing up, I mainly followed those of my parents and my family. As I became more independent and moved away to university, I met a broader range of people, which made me consider my own values and beliefs. I was introduced to new ideas and realised that where other people had led lives quite different to my own, it didn't make one right and the other wrong, they were just different. I think the majority of people share the same core values, they believe it is wrong to take the life of another human being, or to steal from someone else or to hurt them physically. I would like to think that I treat others how I would like to be treated myself. However, like everyone else, I am not perfect (far from it), so whilst this may be my philosophy, so to speak, I don't always manage to do this. It's hard to write about this objectively, but maybe a less controversial example might be politics. For instance, if two people have widely differing political beliefs, then the likelihood is they will find it difficult to get on without some degree of conflict. I suppose the chances are, if you find someone else's beliefs, morals and values to be vastly different or unpalatable, then you would not want to enter into a relationship with them.

I think this is where being friends beforehand can be helpful. You have time to get to know the person, to discover on some level whether they are reliable and trustworthy, whether you have anything in common.

It may seem strange not to have put this in at the start, but I will also mention:

- attraction

- love

- compromise

- communication.

How come I didn't mention these before? Well, communication is not my forte because I find it hard to recognise and describe my emotions. One thing I have learned is that this is probably the most important element in a relationship, although personally I would place it after trust and values. Then again, that's maybe where the trust comes from, but I don't know the answer to that.

Communication, or rather the lack of it, has probably been the most problematic part of my relationship, both in terms of the effect it has had and the difficulties it presents. There have been countless occasions in the past where I have been asked what is wrong. Sometimes I wasn't aware that anything was wrong, but other times, I just didn't know what it was, or I didn't know how to describe what I was feeling and I couldn't see that I was reacting to a situation in what appeared to other people as a totally unreasonable and irrational way. The fact that I then would not or could not talk about it made the situation far worse. In fact, it became more of an issue than the problem itself. I would be asked to explain how I was feeling and why I wasn't saying anything. I tried desperately to think of something to say, but my mind seemed to go blank, I simply didn't know what to say and I think it came across as I didn't care. I was often left thinking, where did all of this come from, how come I am in this situation?

Personally I don't class a person's physical appearance as being high on my list of priorities with regards to any form of relationship. In terms of a personal relationship, though, it may be possible that there are some people I would find physically unattractive or unappealing enough to make me not want to go out with them. I find, however, it is how a person treats me and how they make me feel that is most important. I believe there has to be some level of physical attraction, and recognise that for some people this will be very important, although whether that leads to a successful and lasting relationship I don't know.

In terms of physical contact, it very much depends on the individual. Some people enjoy a lot of physical contact, whereas others may be tactile defensive. My daughter says hugging me is sometimes like hugging a coat stand, whilst at other times I enjoy being close. I think this is definitely a matter for consideration.

I know I have been looking at relationships more from the point of sustaining them and what I believe makes a relationship successful. However, I think for the majority of people, with or without Asperger syndrome, the first question is, how do I meet someone in the first place? I'm not going to say too much on the subject as I'm sure there are many people with far more experience and knowledge than myself. When I met David internet dating did not exist, however, I do believe it can be quite a successful way to meet someone, especially where people are matched according to their expectations and values. However, one thing I think it is important to mention, however you may meet a potential partner, it is unlikely you will meet your 'ideal' or 'perfect' partner, particularly first time round. That isn't to say it can't or won't happen but, if that is what you are expecting, then you may be sorely disappointed or disheartened. You may both have to be prepared to make some compromises in order to make things work. You may need to look at what your priorities are, in much the same way as if you were contemplating buying a house (i.e. there will be aspects you would definitely want to have and others which you would like but would be prepared to forgo), and you need to feel comfortable with your decision. I apologise if this isn't a very romantic way of looking at relationships, but then I am not that kind of person, I am more of a realist, I guess and I am looking at it from a practical point of view.

Another point I would like to make is that both myself and David have Asperger syndrome, although we weren't aware of this until a few years ago. I would say this has both helped and hindered our relationship in some ways. I think what I liked about him in the first place is the fact that he was honest and he always had lots of interesting things to talk about; I never felt like I was having to try to think of something to say or felt awkward or uncomfortable in his company. He also seemed very kind, and liked me the way I was. I never felt I had to pretend to be anything other than how I am. As we got to know one another better, we discovered that we both liked some quite wacky things and we share a similar sense of humour. We respect each other's differences, and whilst we share some interests, we recognise we have our own interests that we need to pursue. I would like to make the comment here that it did in fact take me some years to come to this realisation and even knowing this, I am not wholly tolerant or understanding.

Although I recognise that people can be very different, from my own perspective, I feel that my lack of self-esteem has had quite an impact on our relationship. This means that I often have a rather pessimistic and negative outlook on life, which I guess can become a little tedious, and can be difficult to live with. One of the main misunderstandings we have is the fact that I often assume other people are cross or angry with me. Often it transpires they are just upset or angry about something in general, but I am almost always convinced that it is me they are angry with, yet I don't know what I have done to upset them. This leads to frustration and upset on both sides.

A relationship is supposed to be a two-way process. There will be times when either person may require more emotional support due to what is happening in their lives. I find that sometimes the reason for this is not immediately obvious to me. However, from experience, I think you have to accept that this is the situation and try to help the other person through it by listening to them and asking them if there is anything you can do to help. Sometimes they may just want a hug or someone to talk to, to know that someone cares about them and is there for them. Sometimes they don't want to have to explain, they want you to know instinctively, but unfortunately you can't always know.

In addition, I will also mention:

- romance/romantic gestures

- companionship

- time alone.

Much seems to be made of celebrating Valentine's Day, of buying presents and cards for specific occasions to demonstrate how romantic you are. Where there is an expectation to do this, it can be quite stressful. Personally, I would rather buy a gift for someone when I see something I think they will really like, or if it is something I think they will appreciate. Fairly early on in our relationship we decided that we didn't like the idea of having to conform to buying cards and gifts that to us weren't very meaningful. I feel that gestures such as cooking a meal, or bringing home a shiny new conker or a pretty stone which I will appreciate are far more meaningful. However, I do feel it is important to establish what your partner's expectations are, otherwise they may end up being quite disappointed or even take it to mean that you don't care. Likewise, really they should also take your views into consideration. Some people enjoy receiving bunches of flowers and boxes of chocolates, quite why I don't know, and whether they really do other than because it is expected due to social pressure, who knows. Also, remembering to buy someone a card and flowers which you can buy at just about any shop or garage hardly makes you romantic. Maybe I am confusing romantic gestures with being helpful or supportive but, to me, if I come home from work and my husband says he is making tea, or he has done something I'm not looking forward to doing, then that to me shows that he cares and makes me feel better and happier. Maybe it's not so much confusing being romantic with being caring, it's just that I consider that to be more important to me than romance or romantic gestures. I think I view life in a more practical way and, therefore, being shown kindness, consideration and understanding is far more meaningful to me.

I will mention companionship and solitude together. From my understanding many people with Asperger syndrome need time alone, whether to process information or to unwind and de-stress. Sometimes it's good to spend time absorbed in an activity, however, at some point you are likely to feel lonely and would like some company. For some people, a purely platonic relationship may be all they require but, for the majority of people, they will want a closer relationship. I think it is important for a partner to understand this aspect so that they don't see it as rejection or a lack of interest in themselves. They may also be close to family or friends and see a lot of them, and it may not be something you can deal with. David and I have reached an understanding whereby I don't always accompany him to see his family or, if his brother calls round, I don't need to be there all the time and they understand/accept that sometimes I don't feel in the mood for socialising.

I also feel it is important to add that a relationship is about the two people involved, and so long as you are both happy within the parameters of your relationship, and you are in agreement with how it works for both of you, then there is no right or wrong way to conduct your relationship. Some people would like to have children, whereas others may not. Disagreeing over this can cause serious conflict in a relationship, and it is better to establish what both of you would prefer where a relationship is developing into something more serious. Again, whether to have children or not is a personal preference and there are many aspects to consider, it's not just about doing what everyone one else is doing because it is expected. It's a commitment to put another person first for what may be the rest of your life. Yes, a child becomes an adult in law at the age of 18, and most people would like to achieve at least some level of independence if they can, but that person is still your child and they may need your support. Of course, having your own family can provide a lot of happiness, I am merely pointing out the practicalities.

Before I finish, I would like to say that some people may be perfectly happy to remain single. The main thing really is for the individual to feel happy and comfortable with the situation they are in.

I asked my husband David if there was anything he would like to add. His contribution is to say, when you enter into a relationship, be aware that people can and sometimes do change, maybe for the better, maybe for the worse, and it is never a good idea to enter into a relationship with the intention of changing someone to fit the profile of your ideal partner.

Chapter 13

Building and Maintaining an Intimate Relationship

Dr Christopher Wilson

Introduction by Dean Worton

Christopher is a personal friend of mine. He is a highly organised individual who comes across as confident in social situations and is successful in his career. However, as he mentions there always comes a time in each day when he needs downtime away from other people. In a relationship it is almost always necessary to spend large amounts of time with the other person and to show various behaviours that might not really be you! In fact, some of the emotional and romantic gestures expected in relationships are very uncomfortable for many with Asperger syndrome (AS), and could require putting on an act. Many AS individuals including Christopher are very straightforward and do not want to do that! It seems rather crazy that human nature is so at odds with this honesty. It's a strange world when you think about it!

Introduction

My name is Christopher Wilson; I am 28 years old and have lived all of my life in Chorley, Lancashire. Although, I have both AS and dyslexia I am proud to say that it has not affected large parts of my life. I am employed as a private sector consultant undertaking research in the areas of town planning and urban regeneration, on behalf of local councils. In the course of this I have to undertake any number of social interactions, from telephone interviews to chairing meetings and making short presentations (usually) without problems. Prior to this I undertook a doctorate at Manchester University, which included an element of teaching. Again, I could do it successfully, even if I did not always enjoy it.

However, one aspect of my life which I have always struggled with is the building and maintaining of an intimate relationship. I have had four relationships in my life which I would describe as intimate. Each has lasted between four weeks and five months, before ending in a break-up. Although it is valid for me to say that I have not yet found the 'right woman', with whom I wish to spend the rest of my life, I must also acknowledge those aspects of my personality which have made building and maintaining an intimate relationship more difficult.

Generally, I am a person who dislikes intense displays of emotion in anybody. Even in TV programmes and films I tend to switch over, when people (who are obviously acting) are having an emotional scene. I never watch programmes such as *Big Brother*, which seem to rely almost exclusively on emotion for entertainment. This carries over into my relationships, where I have often had trouble empathising with the emotions of my partner. Even with women I have cared about deeply it has been very hard for me to be sympathetic over what often seemed like trivial things to get upset about. Since I would be unlikely to bother about (or even notice) a word or gesture out of place, it has always been hard not to hold others to the same standard. Understandably, my partners have seen this as a lack of empathy and emotional intelligence on my part.

For example, one of my ex-girlfriends was unhappy that I kept up (platonic) friendships with two girls I had known at university, while dating her. These were two longstanding friends, and her jealous reaction seemed childish in the extreme. Whatever the rights and wrongs of the issue, it was very hard for me to see what the problem was or why I should be sympathetic to (what seemed to me) a gross overreaction. It was therefore my lack of sympathy, as much as the original problem, which helped to spoil the relationship.

Linked to this is body language. Difficulties with body language is something that almost all those with AS have problems with and this can impact on intimate relationships in ways that are often difficult to predict. For example, during a recent relationship my girlfriend and I were walking to a pub holding hands. At one point she became annoyed that I was holding hands 'incorrectly' (i.e. with my hand at the back and hers at the front). Apparently, the man was supposed to have his hand at the front so he is effectively 'leading' the woman. At the time I was annoyed at this, how was I expected to know there was a right way and wrong way to hold hands?! Why would anyone care about something so trivial?! The answer, of course, is that she cared, regardless of what I or anyone else thought about it.

Finally, there is the issue of commitment, particularly the commitment of time. Although I am not particularly committed to a set daily routine, as some Aspies can be, I do like my privacy. When spending time with friends or family, regardless of whether I am having a good time, there will always come a point when I have just had enough and want to go and spend some time by myself. This is in part due to the challenges of interacting with others, faced by myself and most others with AS (maintaining the tenure of conversation, maintaining eye contact, remembering the appropriate social gestures, etc.). Socialising is, to put it simply, hard work and there always comes a time when I want to take a break.

This has been carried into my intimate relationships as well. Although I have genuinely cared for those who I have had relationships with, and have wanted to be with them, my time apart has also felt just as important to me. This hasn't always been a problem; some of my girlfriends have also wanted personal space. Also circumstances have meant that I have never been able to live with a girlfriend for an extended period. However, it has also been seen as a lack of commitment in a relationship and unwillingness to move to a higher level of intimacy.

So what might I have done differently?

Looking back at my past relationships, I can clearly see a number of traits that made it hard for me to build and maintain an intimate partnership. Although not all are directly the result of my AS, most are traits shared with those with AS and which need to be considered by anybody with AS looking to develop an intimate relationship. Generally, these traits come under four headings:

- empathy

- tolerance

- body language

- commitment.

Empathy

As I mentioned, a perceived lack of empathy has been my big barrier to building and maintaining an intimate relationship. The problem is often that those with AS give the appearance of not caring or being self-absorbed, often combined with minor mistakes that may indicate a lack of empathy to a partner. Some common traits which I have seen in myself and others with AS include:

- discomfort with physical attraction

- difficulty reading non-verbal language

- oversensitivity and obsessing with minor issues in your personal life (thus devoting less attention to your partner's life)

- telling lies to cover up social mistakes (thus breaking trust)

- short attention span (sometimes 'tuning out' what your partner is saying)

- resenting a partner's friendships with others

- difficulty with awareness of the passage of time (i.e. frequently being late when meeting your partner, thus showing a lack of commitment).

More generally, I take a logical approach to relationships, so if a partner comes to me with an upsetting problem, my first instinct is to solve the problem and move on, not provide emotional support. This does not indicate a lack of compassion on my part, rather a desire to put the practical over the emotional.

Such traits will affect any relationship differently, depending both on yourself and what your partner wants out of the relationship, so there is no one solution. However, it is important to understand that opening up your emotional side is part of a developing relationship and that providing comfort and understanding is as important as dealing with practical matters. If some aspect of your behaviour is felt to show a lack of empathy, then you need to discuss it to help your partner understand that it is a genuine problem on your part, not a lack of compassion.

Further, this is one aspect of a relationship where you must 'expect the unexpected'. No matter how open I was or how close to a partner I became, there was always some requirement of my partner's which I couldn't anticipate, some situation where they would have expected me to behave differently to how I did. You may feel your partner is being excessive in focusing on something you consider trivial, while your partner may be unhappy that you did not notice something important to them. However, it is important to have perspective. Such differences are part of any relationship which brings together two distinct individuals. They are not the end of the world and can usually be solved by talking things through.

However, in an equal partnership your partner must also show empathy over your failings. They need to understand, that for someone on the autistic spectrum, just doing the basics of listening, talking, making eye contact and interacting over long periods require a lot of thought. It is not therefore surprising that an individual concentrating on all that may let themselves down in another way, for example by not asking their partner how their day went. No relationship and no interaction will be perfect, and a partner may need to manage their expectations about you, understanding that any failures are not evidence of a lack of love. They are part of what makes you, you.

Tolerance

To engage in an intimate relationship is to open yourself up to another person in a way you have probably never done previously. This will include sharing your personal hopes and fears, your dreams, your prejudices and your most private thoughts. This is not something that will happen overnight; part of building an intimate relationship is the gradual process of learning about each other. And it works both ways; you will be sharing information with your partner and gaining it in return.

Not everything you learn about another person will be pleasant; everyone in the world has views, personal habits, prejudices and aspects of their past which others may find uncomfortable or objectionable. Engaging in an intimate relationship means learning to live together despite the differences. A degree of tolerance is required in any relationship, regardless of whether either partner has AS, however AS does add additional complications.

As a general rule I am quite good at concealing my 'Aspie' traits when interacting with people, others are not. However, in an intimate relationship this is largely irrelevant as these aspects will emerge sooner or later. Indeed, if you are quite good at concealing traits then this creates an additional problem, as in the early stages of a relationship your partner may be unaware of the 'real you'. Only later, as the relationship builds, will they see you 'warts and all', and this becomes a test of whether they are willing to move the relationship on. Sadly, in the case of several of my relationships, my partners were unwilling to do this.

Just what your partner must be willing to 'tolerate' will of course, vary, nor are any negative traits set in stone. Learning what a partner does and does not find acceptable is part of building a relationship, as is working to address the unacceptable things. For myself, the negative traits I displayed in my relationships were fairly clear:

- needing a lot or reassurance

- a need for personal space

- difficulty in discussing feelings and emotions

- lack of empathy with my partner's thoughts and feelings, not showing appropriate interest.

However, tolerance works both ways and if you are engaged in an intimate relationship with someone who is of the predominant neurotype (PNT) then they will have traits that you might have to tolerate. From my own experience these may include:

- excessive reliance on body language such as eye contact to make judgements about you

- easily offended by minor mistakes in social interaction (not keeping such mistakes in perspective)

- a lack of understanding as to how difficult social interaction might be for you

- willingness to disrespect personal space.

If you can build a relationship despite these differences, then you have a bedrock for a strong future together.

Body language

The previous example I gave illustrates that body language is about more than just eye contact. A neurotypical (NT) person may have any number of expectations regarding when and how you interact with them physically, from kissing, hugging and handholding to (seemingly) minor things such as how you stand or sit next to them, look at them and, yes, how you make eye contact. You are unlikely to be able to anticipate all the ways in which your partner may expect you to act in advance, everyone is different. Finding this out (and adapting yourself) is part of growing to understand a person.

However, it is important to help your partner understand that body language is simply not as important to you, and how you view others (including your partner), as it might be. It should not automatically be taken as a lack of affection. Also that, as a person on the autistic spectrum, you are making an effort just by maintaining regular eye contact and undertaking actions y do without thinking. Thus one contribution they could make to an equal partnership is to allow you periods to 'be yourself' and relax in a way you find comfortable, particularly when it is just the two of you.

Commitment

If you are entering into an intimate relationship with someone, then you are, in practice, committing to spend most of your personal time with that person, maybe for the rest of your life. Of course if you have developed strong feelings for that person then you want to spend as much time with them as possible, culminating in living together and potentially marriage. This is a significant commitment for any person to make, and may seem understandably daunting at first, particularly for those on the autistic spectrum.

At its most basic, such a commitment will mean significant changes in lifestyle and in daily routine. Change is something that those on the autistic spectrum are seen to have trouble with. Many with AS (particularly those who have been single for an extended period) will have developed a set routine in their lives which they may be unwilling to break. However, it is important to understand that such change is part of relationships and part of the natural development and growth of a person. Although you may be initially resistant to changing your ways, such changes are rarely as bad as they might first appear, and will often be for the better. It is also important to remember that your partner will be making changes for you, and reciprocating is essential to the development of an equal partnership. The more positive you can be about change, the more easily your relationship will grow.

One of the strongest commitments you will make (and one of the biggest changes) will be to move in with your partner. Perhaps the most daunting aspect of this, for those on the autistic spectrum, will be the loss of personal space (something I had a particular problem with). Until that point, regardless of how much time you spend with that person, there is always a point when you both said goodbye and returned to your own private lives. After that point your private lives will be lived together. This means opening up all aspects of your private personality, your quirks and your bad (and good) habits.

There is no set point in a relationship when living together is considered acceptable, and it will depend on your personal and practical circumstances. A deciding factor might be how much privacy and intimacy you can get living apart, especially if one or more of you lives with family. In my relationships, both my partners and I lived with our families, reducing the time we could be alone together, without going out. However, neither of us could afford to move out and, as I have mentioned, this had advantages for me at the time. Regardless, it is important to remember the level of commitment it entails, and to talk it through with your partner beforehand.

Living together is a significant step, but also a positive one; it is the final test of whether you are compatible in the long term. It allows you to see your partner 'warts and all' and may allow you to make the further commitment of getting married.

Chapter 14

Thoughts from a Late-Diagnosed Aspie...and from Her Husband Too...

Joanna Treasure and Jon[1]

Introduction by Dean Worton

It would really be impossible to fully do Jo and Jon's chapter justice in this brief intro. I think we can all agree that it's easier to navigate the world as babies when all our needs are catered for. Even predominant neurotypes (PNTs) have to work hard to look after themselves but they get there somehow. Despite many hard times that Jo has experienced throughout her life, she has always managed to keep going. She is a very interesting lady to be around and can be pleasurable company. Although Jo's husband Jon is not on the autistic spectrum it is clear from his input to this chapter that he appreciates her for who she is. As you read the chapter, although a lot of banter is used, it seems good hearted and by the end hopefully you'll wish that there were more PNTs like Jon in the world.

---

1   Please note: This chapter is written by a married couple. Jo has Asperger syndrome, and Jon is not on the autistic spectrum. Most of this article is written by Jo, but throughout the chapter are responses written within speech marks by Jon.

Romance can be the most wonderful, inspirational, magical and motivating energy to experience!

But it can also be just too emotionally draining an experience to want to engage in it.

Romance is inherently unpredictable – a metaphorical minefield – and it's tricky enough for anybody to get through it unhurt, even if you don't live with the additional complications of having difficulties with social communication, social interaction and social imagination, as we Aspies may.

As the saying goes, 'The path to true love never did run smooth.' For all the thrills of mutual attraction and shared excitement at the prospect of each other's company, which can be enhanced and celebrated by the exchanging of tokens such as Valentine's cards, flowers, gifts or other social niceties associated with courtship, there are risks associated with any attempts at being romantic.

> Jon: '…"never did run smooth". Hitting difficulties in relationships is very common. I'd been married and divorced myself, years before we met at the dance club. I reckon we'd both given up on ever finding a partner again, let alone going steady and starting a family. What first attracted me to you was your smile. You dance well – but it's the fact that you enjoy it so much – you really come to life on that dance floor!'

Couples may find themselves out of synch, having differing expectations from one another so that perhaps one person is expecting a romantic gesture but the other person has no idea that one is expected, or one party may embarrass the other by displays of affection which are regarded as excessive or inappropriate. All of those ups and downs can be so unsettling. They can be enough to prevent a relationship from getting going in the first place, or they can lead to dissatisfaction and kill off the romance – either for both or sometimes sadly for only one, whilst the other pines and grieves.

> Jon: 'The fact that you don't like surprises is OK with me. You prefer to choose your own treats.'

For many people, the combination of mating instincts and a yearning for loving companionship may amount to a long-term source of stress and distress – with the excitement of meeting someone new followed all too soon by the emotional crises of breaking up. Some become obsessed. They may struggle to judge what is OK and what is not, or to realise when their attentions are not wanted. They may get it so wrong that they lay themselves open to allegations of stalking or harassment, which must be devastating, especially if they had no idea of how badly it was going wrong. Others have terrible problems of jealousy.

It's enough to cause us to look back to the relative simplicity of our childhoods with longing!

> Jon: 'Slow down a minute, Jo! They're looking for a chapter, not a thesis on stalkers!'

When we start off, as newborn babes, we are entirely dependent upon the grown ups who care for us, giving us food and security. As long as they attend to our needs, we are happy. As we grow up we become increasingly aware of our place in the community, and we need to make effective working relationships within school and society, as well as making friends. All that can be plenty enough to keep us busy...and then adolescence sets in – and nature plays a cheeky trick on us. We rapidly evolve into Hormone Factories, beset with urges that can take us by surprise in so many ways, however much we try to moderate them and to control our own behaviour, as we aspire to become decent members of adult society.

Those turbulent teenage years are particularly challenging years for all human beings.

Jon: 'Fun too though – at least for some of the time – and I feel proud to see our boys growing up.'

We may develop romantic attachments in all sorts of unsuitable directions – or find that others are inconveniently becoming romantically attached to us. Even though the emotional rollercoaster ride may even out over time as we adapt to adulthood and to the various different challenges we face, these romantic feelings may continue to confuse and distract us as long as we are single and open to the idea of dating – and even sometimes when we think we are not. If we are fortunate, we may eventually meet suitable partners and find the support to settle down into partnership, perhaps marriage, and perhaps starting families of our own.

'And they lived happily ever after...'. Well, that is the final phrase of so many fairy tales – but anyone who embarks on married life thinking that all the important work is now done and finished is very badly mistaken! Unfortunately, the high divorce rates in our Western societies tend to suggest that many couples do tend to have this mistaken attitude to their intimate relationships so that they are surprised when they become disillusioned and may give up far too easily.

The honest truth is that all relationships need constant work and attention if they are to flourish – or even survive. If you have found a good relationship, though, it really is worth giving it that care and attention.

Jon: 'Agreed. We both put a lot of thought into our marriage – and we must be doing something right as we're still together (so far at least).'

So, how does it affect things if one of you is autistic, with Asperger syndrome?

I've been invited to contribute a piece for this book on the grounds that I have been diagnosed with Asperger syndrome. Inevitably, this can only be a very personal perspective. Each Asperger's personality and life experience will be unique to the individual. My account may be very different from that of an 'archetypal loner' Aspie who struggles to make eye contact let alone express or relate to emotional intimacy – and when we think of that archetype it will usually be a male that we envisage, but that doesn't mean that women are immune from relationship angst – certainly not!

Women may be programmed in ways that enable those of us who are Asperger women (or Aspergirls) more often to *appear* more adept at such aspects of social interactions – but the underlying social imagination and communication difficulties are still there, along with our Aspie tendencies to intense analysing, systematising, pedantry and perfection-ism, as well as an inclination to pursue passionate interests with intense focus more easily than to engage in the superficial topics of conversation which predominantly neurotypical society tends to use.

Jon: 'What did I say about not writing a thesis?'

It has to be acknowledged that Aspies may often find it hard to get along with people in general. In contrast, my husband gets along very well with most people. He is generally affable and good natured.

Jon: 'OK I'll have that.'

It so happens that I was diagnosed late in life – after I'd already been living with my husband for 15 years and married to him for ten. It was after Asperger's was identified in one of our sons that my own diagnosis came to light, at the age of 50. This means that I'd been living my whole life up until that point without having realised that Asperger syndrome explains so much about my own life history – always feeling like a misfit at parties or in social groups within school, even at primary school age; not being sure of how to act under different circumstances; forming an impression that there was some set of rules about how one was supposed to behave but that the rest of the community had somehow just not been kind enough to share them with me – all the difficulties that other 'Aspergirls' have written about.

I was clever enough, and adaptable enough, to hide it. I must have hidden it well, because no one spotted it for all of those decades. (Or, rather, if any did spot it, they didn't point it out to me clearly enough for me to realise.) (I think at least one thoughtful person may have tried to point it out to me, but when I started to read books and websites on the subjects, I still wasn't able to identify it in myself. Subsequently, I realised that this was because the 'thumbnail sketch' generally described just didn't appear to fit me well enough. However, since I have learnt about the more feminine styles of presentation, and learnt more about autism and Asperger's in general, I now realise how very accurately it applies to me, and how well it explains my life's experiences.)

> Jon: 'If you didn't know about it, I certainly didn't. I just knew I was glad to have met you.'

So, it was something that was essentially hidden. I overcame any associated problems as best as I could, often very successfully, and I hid symptoms and signs that might have made the diagnosis more apparent, all motivated by wanting to please others, to please my teachers, to fit into society.

It turns out that that's how a lot of us manage the condition. We want to fit in, of course we do! And, if we can, we do – despite the enormous and incredibly exhausting effort involved.

Social interactions are important to all of us, right from babyhood upwards. We need to have the approval of our parents and carers, of our teachers in school, our schoolmates (or at least to try not to be teased or rejected by them), our trainers, our employers and of any other adult associates in whatever spheres of activities we become involved in. So we do our best to fit in as best we can and that's how we live our lives, putting on an act of fitting in, copying how to behave, watching everyone really closely so as to notice when we are getting it wrong and quickly adapting if we can do so. That is, if we can do so.

Aspies like me, who are observant enough, quick-thinking enough, adaptable enough, do so.

That's how we manage to look more or less like we are fitting in, for the majority of the time at least, as if we are normal, like the predominantly neurotypical majority surrounding us.

Of course, for most of my life, I had no idea that this was what was going on, at the time.

In retrospect, it all begins to make sense.

Thinking back to my 20s, I remember a very good friend saying to me, 'Just be yourself, Jo.' The conversation moved on without any specific comment from me, and yet I remember thinking at the time, 'Well, *that's* not going to work!' I have always been vulnerable to criticism. I have always lacked confidence and struggled with low self-esteem. Kind people tried to help by offering advice such as 'You've just got to develop a thicker skin,' but that advice always struck me as unworkable.

During my 40s, when I took evening classes in Counselling Theory and Practice (levels 2 and 3), one of the self-awareness exercises alerted me to the fact that I tend to have an 'external locus of approval', meaning that I tend to be more influenced by and concerned about what others think of me than by my own self-appraisal...and I've always felt that this was somehow a weakness or failing on my part. Throughout various counselling relationships, as well as during all the other efforts I've made towards personal development, I have noticed that, however much I study and reflect upon my own personality, behaviour and choices in life, I still feel a deep-seated need to run my ideas past others that I consider as appropriate mentors and advisors. I have tended to see this being intrinsic to my sense of inadequacy and had always tended to see this as somehow my fault, an inadequacy that was part of my own responsibility, somehow causing and perpetuating my vulnerabilities to depression and anxiety.

I now realise that that was a ridiculously unjust distortion of the truth!

However, even since discovering my identity as an Aspergirl, it has taken me months to realise so!

Gradually, it has dawned on me that, as 'being myself' was considered so unacceptable to general society, it was only through moderating my behaviour, and changing it towards something more 'convenient' and 'socially acceptable', that I have managed to fit in as well as I have. Any success I've had in overcoming the difficulties associated with my 'hidden disability' is attributable to the fact that I am willing to acquiesce to the opinions of others and moderate my behaviour accordingly.

That is the secret of my success! ...as well as accounting for my repeated perceptions of failure.

It is a 'Catch 22' kind of thing.

> Jon: 'The first evening we had a proper date, away from the dance club, you told me your whole life story pretty much. You talked about how much of a struggle it's been at times. I just felt impressed at your resilience and the fact that you keep persevering, trying to be as content and as good company and as productive as you can manage.

Nineteen years later, I've learnt a lot more about it. We've gone through good times and bad. I've seen you in a variety of moods – and I think I understand a lot more now – but I realise I won't ever fully appreciate your perspective on things.'

So, what happens when we don't manage to keep up the act?

What happens if we just get so exhausted and stressed by the strain and effort of keeping up the illusion to the best of our abilities but the cracks keep showing, and then all we seem to get is criticism for not having managed to behave nicely – as if we were not even trying!

After all, as there may be no one aware that we have this Asperger's thing to contend with (not even ourselves), no one knows that, in all fairness, there may be good reason to justify making extra allowances for any behaviours that are less than welcome.

This, in essence, is the *exquisite torture* of living with a hidden disability. As long as our difficulties are unrecognised, we get no credit for overcoming them. Whatever effort we put into overcoming our problems remains unnoticed, as long as we are being reasonably successful at it. However, when we struggle or fail to compensate for them, we get rebuked and criticised – because no one realises how hard we've had to work at it in order to go 'below the radar' up until that point at which our strategies are all overwhelmed and the cracks begin to show…

To say that this can be disheartening is a *massive* understatement.

Over the years, over the decades, it can become gradually devastating to be trying so hard to get on with people, to fit into social circles, to be a good friend, only to face repeated examples of relationships going wrong despite your best efforts. Or perhaps, in a way, *because* of your best efforts –

because you have social difficulties maybe you are trying too hard at your relationships, which may mean that they are never going to work naturally.

It can also be chronically disabling to face incessant teasing, mocking or criticism – which could be brushed off by more robust individuals but when you are so vulnerable to it, it can amount to subtle but persistent bullying...and it is a cause of chronic post-traumatic stress disorder.

All of this is bound to affect our intimate relationships too. After all, if Asperger's is to do with having difficulty with social communication, social interaction and social imagination, it's certain to have an impact on our romantic relationships just as much as on any other kind of relationship.

The big difference, however, is the amount of commitment invested in a romantic relationship.

When two people love each other enough to make a true commitment to the relationship whatever the difficulties, there is every opportunity to work through their difficulties, to share their feelings and experiences, and to find compromises and adaptations which can work for both of them.

> Jon: 'That's what keeps us together, I reckon. A combination of commitment – and stubbornness.'

Vulnerability to mental health problems

I've had difficulties with my mental health for most of my adult life. Autism is not necessarily associated with mental health problems – but it so often may be – whether due to the result of being mocked, teased and bullied, simply on account of being different from average, or whether due to the sheer exhaustion of constantly trying to conceal your true self and hide or compensate for your idiosyncratic characteristics.

My mood varies a lot, depending on circumstances.

My first referral to a psychiatrist was in my early 20s. This was for depression with anxiety accompanied by significant suicidal ideation, a tendency which keeps recurring, despite everything I do to try to keep it away.

It wasn't the first time I'd been depressed. Looking back, I feel I can identify episodes of blue moods right back to my primary school years, but they probably weren't persistent. During my early years at secondary school, I certainly did experience a lot of anxiety, partly because of being bullied a bit and having to learn how to deal with that without any help, as I didn't talk to anybody else about it, seeing it as my own problem due to a weakness on my own part.

My adolescence was characterised by extreme self-consciousness, which was potentially very debilitating – but I am an intelligent, thoughtful, reflective individual who has routinely invested a lot of thought into managing my difficulties. I observed what was going on around me in minute detail. I noticed what people did and I copied their behaviour so that I would pass as normal.

When I had to go into a completely strange and unfamiliar situation, I felt almost overwhelmed by social anxiety and became so self-conscious that I would tend to imagine that everybody would be able to tell how much I was struggling with my nerves – but I was resourceful! I managed the situation by purposefully inventing a series of activities to occupy myself during those crucial early minutes, so that it would always look to anyone as if I was busy doing something. That way, I was able to reassure myself that if anyone looked at me, they would just see someone who was busy doing something, and no one would be able to guess how I felt inside! This enabled me to cope with the situation until it was time for the event to start – and overcoming my self-consciousness felt good.

This is how it always was. Struggling inside, almost as a routine way of life, but doing my best to be the best possible version of myself. This included learning to appreciate myself all the more through valuing every step I made towards fitting in and being appreciated or, at least, accepted by others.

Part of human development involves comparing one's own perspective with whatever we imagine to be the perspective of others. Realistically speaking, I suppose that adolescence is a time when all human beings are particularly vulnerable to self-consciousness. Still, at some stage, as I began to guess that it was harder for me than it seemed to be for most others around me, this only would have reinforced my sense of inadequacy, low confidence and low self-esteem, which has become such a persistent feature of my entire adult life.

Since the first time I left home for university, I have had a recurrent tendency to anxiety (at first and occasionally since even amounting to panic attacks). By the time I was in my final year, working flat out, and on multiple occasions since then, depression has been the major blight on my life. Looking back, I do believe I have experienced a significant degree of depression, with anxiety, over the majority of my adult life.

Many people would not have been aware of the extent to which I was struggling with depression.

Since I had no choice but to continue to earn my living, I would turn up for work each day and smile at people, exchange in social pleasantries according to the local customs and find great comfort in turning my focus of attention onto my work. Having the Asperger ability to compartmentalise quite efficiently, through the intense focus of attention that we may bring to bear on the specific subject which requires it at any given time, meant that my work was like occupational therapy, distracting me from depressive ruminations which would otherwise torment me, as they did during my evenings and weekends. Going to work kept me going!

This naturally involved putting on a performance throughout each working day – but wasn't that exactly what I'd had to do throughout my life in any case, just in order to look and behave as if I was a predominantly neurotypical person! Acting the part is what I had become good at, through sheer necessity of survival.

> Jon: 'When I first met you, in the dance club, I was attracted to your lovely smile and engaging personality. I had no idea you were badly depressed at the time.'

During most of my life, I've had to put a lot of effort into trying to keep mental health issues at bay, and most of my strategies have centred around finding the most constructive blend of work, study and recreation I could achieve. With problems of low self-esteem and high anxiety, even during the good times, I've tended to feel a need to keep busy and active, so that if problems arise in one area of life, there is at least a chance of finding enjoyment in another area. That meant that I could at least comfort myself that I was doing the best I could under the circumstances and making the most productive use of any time available.

When I have found the depression, anxiety or general stress to be getting on top of me, I have found counselling very supportive and beneficial. I have paid privately for several courses of long-term counselling on a weekly or fortnightly basis. These were generally of the Rogerian, humanistic, person-centred school – based on the principle that the client has the best answers within themselves, whilst the role of the counsellor is to enable the client to identify their own answers to problems through providing empathy, congruence and unconditional positive regard.

Cognitive therapy has also been a life-saver, on many occasions, since 1989. Following a recommendation, I taught it to myself from the excellent self-help manual by David Burns, *Feeling Good – The New Mood Therapy*.[2]

During 1995–6, I underwent Brief Structured Therapy at Gaskell House in Manchester under the National Health Service, which was delivered within a respectful, considerate, supportive and caring context, thanks to Dr M. and Dr A. Personally, I very much believe that the quality of the therapeutic relationship is absolutely crucial, if there is to be any hope of a constructive effect. (Subsequently, I have been told that some psychotherapists apparently don't think it matters, but I don't understand how or why any 'school of thought' would have adopted such a view.)

In 2012, following my Asperger diagnosis, I count myself extremely lucky to have received a course of Solution Focused Therapy with Vicky Bliss.[3] After a few sessions, I began to notice how easy and pleasant it felt, surprisingly enjoyable, so that it was easy to look forward to the sessions and I didn't feel like I was doing any real work. Once I noticed that, I began to doubt whether there could be any real therapeutic value in it – until I bought her book and read it from start to finish – and very soon realised why I was feeling so much better without even noticing.

Vicky was doing Solution Focused Therapy – and it was brilliantly effective. The focus was not on the problem, but on the solutions – things I was already doing – strengths and resiliences that I was already using in other aspects of my life that I could bring into play to help reduce the problem further – and, all the while, steadily undoing some of the damage that had been done to my self-esteem by the many years of problem-orientated approaches.

In most therapies the client is encouraged to focus on the problem and work towards trying to make it go away.

---

2   Burns, D. (1999) *Feeling Good – The New Mood Therapy*. New York: Avon Books.

3   Brief Therapy Support Services Ltd. Available at http://btss.org.uk, accessed on 8 August 2016.

That carries significant disadvantages when so much of our problems are really due to being treated 'unkindly' simply because we stand out as different from average people. That difference is so intrinsic to our personalities that there is no way it is going to go away.

Some of the most well-intentioned interventions being promoted appear to centre around aiming to make the features associated with autism become less apparent. That kind of approach may potentially involve repression and even oppression. I have serious concerns about whether such treatments, carried out with the best of intentions but also with noticeable passion and intensity, may sometimes be misguided, inappropriate or even abusive.

Diagnosticians are brought up within the problem-orientated model. That fact is clear when you look at the deficit-orientated language of the diagnostic process – including descriptions of the triple deficit model[4] – and the traditional and still widespread terminology of 'autism spectrum disorder'. (Still widespread – but it begins to seem pretty old-fashioned to many of us nowadays.) The use of the 'disorder' word within 'ASD' shows that the approach is 'problem-orientated'.

By using the word 'disorder' practitioners are showing themselves to be at risk of viewing all of the autistic aspects of an autistic personality as if they are problems. That is an extremely limited and limiting view because it misses the fact that many of the autistic features are readily seen to be positively advantageous, when viewed in an appropriate context.

---

4   By 'triple deficit model' I intended to refer to the 'Triad of Social
      Impairments', as described for autism in 1979 by Lorna Wing and
      Judith Gould, including impairments of social interaction, of
      social language and communication and of social imagination. See
      Wing, L. and Gould, J. 'Severe impairments of social interaction
      and associated abnormalities in children: Epidemiology and
      classification.' Journal of Autism and Developmental Disorders, 9, 1, 11–29.

Autistic characteristics are not problems that can be got rid of. They are not going to 'go away'. The autism itself won't 'go away'. It is now recognised as a lifelong neurodevelopmental condition.

I am one of those 1 per cent or so who are identifiably different from the average kind of person, in a number of ways, by which the identification of autism can be made. That's absolutely fine if my differences are valued and appreciated or, at least, accepted. However, most psychiatric and medical approaches are firmly entrenched within a problem-orientated model – a model which tends to suggest you were once normal and, if you cooperate with the recommended treatment with proper compliance and commitment then it should be possible to become normal once more – but if you don't manage it, it must have been your lack of proper compliance and commitment. That's not actually going to work for autistic people though!

Good mental health in Asperger's may not look like that of a neurotypically developed individual, so assessing us in comparison with a fixed idea of normality may be a highly misleading starting point.

Since my autistic spectrum condition has come to light, I have been open in disclosing my diagnosis to many types of professionals interacting with me and other members of my family. I have found it remarkable how very little understanding most mental health service practitioners seem to have about autism and Asperger syndrome, and how pervasive an impact it has on one's entire life. Many professionals haven't yet begun to appreciate just how very difficult and exhausting it can be for us Aspies to take part in conversations, to absorb information and to maintain normal-appearing behaviour when experiencing mounting levels of stress and confusion.

I'm not blaming them. As a trained and qualified doctor myself, and one who has had a lifelong fascination in all things psychological, I had personally believed that

I knew all I needed to know about autism and Asperger's – but I didn't even know enough to manage to diagnose it in myself. So, I have every sympathy with the mental health professionals – and will continue to do so, as long as they are willing to be respectful enough – and modest enough – to try to understand more about autistic conditions and what it is like for us to live with them.

Psychiatric theory and practice appears to be firmly locked into a categorisation of mental illness which is steeped in traditional and very slowly evolving concepts. So much so that I wonder whether the classification system is sufficiently flexible to accommodate concepts as recent as Asperger syndrome. Autism doesn't seem to fit within the psychiatric differential diagnosis – but trying to fit autistic people into the currently available set of psychiatric diagnoses doesn't seem the best way to go about trying to help us maintain good mental health.

My impression of psychiatric theory and practice is that it tends to presume that mental health patients were probably once normal, but developed mental health problems either in response to psychologically damaging experiences during childhood or in response to life events occurring either then or since: the problem-orientated model presumes that patients have developed problems which need fixing. As autism is some sort of neurodevelopmental condition which is characterised by various features, traits and personality quotient scores lying outside of the 'normal' range, and which is of lifelong duration, it's just not going to work to try to make us normal! It's not going to happen! The more forcefully you try, the more we may resist – or, the more we may crumple. Either way, we may find ourselves in conflict with the very people who are sincerely trying to help us – and at times when we are at our most vulnerable and most desperately in need of help, support and understanding. What a nightmare.

Many times, we are living such a nightmare.

I wish that more of the mental health professionals would be more open to finding out more about Asperger's and autism – perhaps by attending conferences such as the one I attended in 2013: 'Autism and Mental Health Conditions' hosted by the National Autistic Society. In the entire packed hall, it turned out that only one psychiatrist was present amongst the delegates! I believe we need to urge psychiatrists to become more actively engaged with the latest insights gained by those who are really familiar with Asperger syndrome in practice.

Due to recurrent depression, I have been dependent on antidepressants for many years now, as well as relying on the support and care of a series of excellent GPs, for which I am very grateful.

Back in 1991, at the age of 31, I had first been prescribed a low dose of Seroxat antidepressant, when I presented to a GP with a full-blown atypical (masked) depression with anxiety, a year or more after my mother's sudden death from a stroke. That medication was really helpful in reducing my anxiety...but I was so very sleepy on it that even the Prof had commented on my yawning. I felt this was not helping my career...so the GP put me on Clomipramine – a tried and tested tricyclic antidepressant. Subsequently, Sertraline was added to that in combination. (As a selective serotonin re-uptake inhibitor or 'SSRI', Sertraline effectively slows down the recycling of the neurotransmitters in the neural synapses...which makes the most of whatever is there.

I'd been pretty stable on a low dose of it for years. On a few occasions, we'd tried to wean me off it, but I just relapsed into suicidal depression so I wasn't in a hurry to repeat that. However, there was some concern about taking it without a mood stabiliser, because it can trigger hypomania in those who are susceptible, so I'd chosen to reduce the dose very very gradually and see if I could do without it altogether. Part of the reasoning was that I'd become fearful that the side effects might be doing me a disservice – by giving me a bit too much confidence – and perhaps making me occasionally appear rude and brash when I didn't intend to have that effect on anyone! I would rather have been thought of as 'lively'. (Please note that this is not me 'tinkering' with my medication. Any changes were made gradually and in consultation with my GP. I felt very lucky that he always listened carefully and respected my right to have an opinion on treatment.)

Last year, though, there were just far too many stressors and too little help and support for me, and by the summer I eventually realised that I was dangerously depressed. I also realised that I probably didn't have any antidepressant on board, which made me even more vulnerable.

It gradually dawned on me that I was experiencing suicidal ideation once more and accepting it as normal – and that I'd run out of tablets some weeks ago, maybe a few months, and only then did I gradually manage to organise myself to get back under the care of my GP and back onto the tablets. It seems to me that I have been on antidepressants for so long now that my brain perhaps simply can't manage without them. Once I got back on a decent dosage again for a couple of weeks, I began to notice signs of physical activity increasing, motivation returning and some enjoyment of experiences once more – so I was able to become hopeful in anticipation of a recovery of a more decent level of mood and satisfaction with life than recently encountered. (Mental note to self: I must try not to let this happen again – it is devastating and potentially highly dangerous.) That was in August 2014. Basically, I was on 'invisible sick leave' for the last six months of 2014 ('invisible' because I am so accustomed to living with and coping with recurrent suicidal ideation that most people are not aware that I am suffering with it, as I go about daily business pretty effectively). I had to put myself on suicide watch for the last four to five months of the year.

Since January 2015 the antidepressants really kicked in with a vengeance, and I found myself struggling to manage symptoms that I realised could easily have been labelled as the 'hypomania' of bipolar disorder (BPD), apart from the fact that I knew (1) they were iatrogenic (meaning 'caused by doctors' – as side effects of the antidepressants) and (2) I was fully aware of what was going on even while I was struggling with the symptoms, and (3) my GP agreed with my evaluation.

The pressure of speech was irrepressible – and embarrassing. I struggled to get enough sleep as I would wake up, wide awake, after only a few hours. It was extremely difficult to keep on task, even despite logging progress against the clock at five-minute intervals. When speaking, I kept going off on tangents and losing my train of thought. My brain felt like porridge with fireworks going off in it. This image was, I'm sure, partly generated by an awareness of the amount of spare serotonin that must be buzzing around in my synapses once the levels of Sertraline had risen so high in my system. My GP and I collaborated to bring the dose back down to zero – but it took three months for the worst of it to ease off. Not a comfortable ride.

Unsurprisingly, without any antidepressant on board, I soon crashed back into despair. We tried using Clomipramine again – but I switched back again into an extremely high state. As soon as I recognised the signs, I stopped the medicine, and things were beginning to settle down again but my GP had gone on leave and was unavailable to help. I was labelled with 'mania' and admitted to hospital under a section 2 (for assessment). Now I've been assigned a diagnosis of 'bipolar disorder', type 2 as the highs were triggered by antidepressant rather than occurring spontaneously.

Jon: 'That was so stressful for both of us – and we weren't given any say in the matter. It seemed as if the decision had already been made before they arrived to assess her. I remember Jo made time to reassure the children, saying that these people wanted her to go into hospital for a while but it would be OK.'

I was allowed out once I'd got started on Lithium, which is a mood stabiliser. Later, when my low mood fell further, my new GP cautiously introduced a different antidepressant called Citalopram. The lethargy and lack of motivation is very debilitating. I feel this is due to the Lithium and I'm hoping it may diminish over time. I'm persevering with it, as well as keeping up as much of my exercise routine as I can – generally four to six sessions a week – as I value exercise as conducive to both physical and mental health.

What about my husband?

Well, what a star he is! My best buddy, my friend, my companion, and a more patient, tolerant, generous-spirited man you could never imagine. If he has any fault at all, it could only be said that he is tolerant to a fault.

If he were not, he would not still be with me.

Every now and then, I catch myself wishing that he were not quite so accepting of me as I am – that he would raise his expectations of me and perhaps do a little more to encourage me to try harder or do better – but then I remember that I always do the best I can to be as well and as productive and as pleasant company as I can be – so if he complained about me it would hardly be fair. And, he doesn't actually tend to complain about anything much.

Also, every now and then, I wish he were not quite so accepting of the problems within our relationship. There are problems, of course, because we are only human. Also, when there are problems, I sometimes wish he could speak up earlier, to tell me what he really thinks and how he really feels. What often tends to happen is that I realise that I'm being mean to him, unreasonable, even, and I realise that he's not happy, but then I have to do a lot of guesswork as to what exactly is bothering him in particular. I then might present options to him according to what I have imagined or guessed that he might be thinking or feeling, so that he has some options to select from, and that can help get the discussion going.

Sometimes I've been really mean to him. That makes me feel ashamed. I still have to keep the faith though, to forgive myself, as well as to be open with him about my regrets.

We've had many happy times together. When I'm 'on good form', I'm the main mover and shaker in the relationship. I tend to take a lead in planning holidays, outings, activities, routines, organisation around the home. He does appreciate it.

He also assures me that he finds me attractive and enjoys my company, and that his life is far better with me than it used to be before we met. That is the best news. It feels very important to me to be reassured that it is so, especially as I struggle even to like myself, when my self-esteem has taken a blow.

At the times when I've been most insecure, whether due to depression or anxiety, I used to say to him, 'Please don't leave me', and he'd say...

Jon: 'I'm not going anywhere. You don't get rid of me that easily.'

Our other favourite saying, which cheers us up during the toughest times, is...

Jon: 'We never said it was going to be easy!'

When I've been on better form, coming around from a low patch, say, he's shared with me more openly about his perspectives on my ever-changing moods. He'd leave for work every morning, do his full shift, then return home, but he would be unable to predict what kind of mood he'd find me in once he got back home to me: that would depend on how my day had gone, what other people may have done or said, or whether I'd been actively engaged and making progress in something or not.

Even leaving aside the varying moods, there have always been some aspects relating to my Asperger personality that have had an impact on our interactions – like the series of passionate interests and intellectual pursuits – and the ever-increasing collections of printed notes and research from my projects and academic studies – collections of materials and resources being accumulated for future use – and various materials being spread around the house only to be left lying around when the next focus for special attention takes over from the last. He's been ever patient with me over such tendencies – too patient really – and, yet, how could he be otherwise if he is to be as understanding and supportive as he is to me?

I usually take a lead on the decision-making process – but I routinely run everything by him. I need his take on things. The process of talking things through with him and carefully considering his responses, including his reactions when I argue points to and fro with him, helps me to navigate through to a decision. He would acknowledge that the final decision may often be ultimately identified by me – and yet I clear any major decisions with him. Once we have talked things through one way and another, we usually come to an agreement between ourselves. Otherwise, we would probably review it again. There is a lot of mutual respect between us and I think that is why we usually come around to a consensus.

There have been times, when we have both been under far too much stress, and on rare occasions, my ability to cope with banter and teasing from him has left me altogether. In retrospect, you could say that that was when my Asperger difficulties with social imagination and social interaction had become most apparent, that I couldn't even cope with teasing from my husband. At those worst times, he would adapt by aiming to be as unambiguous and pedantic as I was being, so that I could be entirely clear as to what we were saying to each other, and teasing was essentially banished for a period of time, until sufficient recovery had taken place to allow us to reintroduce a little banter gradually back into our conversations – and once I was really relaxed and confident again, he would gradually return to his usual slightly flippant style of chat. It is so very welcome when we can return to our normal friendly style of conversation.

There are some aspects of our interactions that are repeatedly mismatched – to do with my difficulties with time management and the strategies I have in place to help me with that. Whereas my husband just identifies what he wants to do that day and gets on and does it, I need to process a complicated system of planning what is coming up over the next few hours, making lists and checking things off, otherwise time drifts by and I may make no progress.

We never quite manage to coordinate smoothly over such differences.

Quite routinely, I will start a Saturday morning off by saying, 'What's on your agenda for today?' and as he replies I will add his priorities to my own checklist. Then he gets up and goes and does it – whereas I'm usually left fuming as I'm still waiting for him to pay me the courtesy of asking the same question back to me. It's daft really, because, if he weren't around, I'd just do my own checklist and get on with prioritising my own list of items for the morning but, with him being there, I somehow expect him to adopt my own strategies with me.

We've discovered a long time ago that it keeps coming as a bit of a surprise to me that he can't actually read my mind and know what I want him to do without me actually telling him.

More recently, I've been having to point out that I can't read *his* mind either. With the amount of strain I've been under, these days, I do find I am constantly asking him to keep working on clarity of communication, and on avoiding ambiguity. He finds it almost impossible to match the extremely logical and pedantic discussion style I tend to adopt when I'm struggling with stress. It's not easy for him, I appreciate. He recognises that it's not easy for me, either.

As we keep making new discoveries, we laugh over them, learn from them, then decide to move on with slightly amended strategies for the future so as to take what we have learnt into account. We keep moving on to fresh examples of equivalent problems – but we keep working at it, and I think that that's what makes our marriage so strong.

That, and the knowledge that we've survived so many tough times – and we are still here, loving each other, despite all of the problems, and enjoying the times in between when we just get along.

Jon: 'And the dancing!'

This was produced in collaboration between Jo and Jon.

Chapter 15

What Makes an Individual the Right Partner?

Lacey Kerr

Introduction by Dean Worton

Lacey's chapter prompts two interesting questions. One is whether a close friend should ever become a partner and the other whether for someone with Asperger syndrome (AS) a relationship would work better with a fellow spectrumite or someone not on the spectrum. I honestly think that there is no firm answer and it's more about the individuals concerned than the closeness of the friendship or any underlying condition. In many cases I suspect AS individuals will have more romantic success if they are open to turning an existing long-term friendship into a relationship, especially as it could for some be almost impossible to create a relationship with anyone they haven't known for long. Ruling it out could turn out to be a tragic decision. Indeed, internet dating is a possible pathway providing that the AS individual is careful about what information they share about themselves and observes personal safety advice. This does however involve a huge time (and cost) commitment.

A fellow AS partner could have more recognition of problems but then not know how to offer the support needed. A predominant neurotypical (PNT) partner might be better at support but not quite grasp exactly what the problems are as they don't have the condition. With pros and cons on both sides I think all one can do is to follow their heart and either the relationship will work or it won't.

I have often thought about my relationships in terms of the positives and negatives. Having only been recently diagnosed with Asperger syndrome at the age of 23, I was able to take another look at my current and past relationships with a fresh point of view (from the eyes of an Aspie). In my case, I have dated an Aspie in the past and I am now currently with a PNT. I have been with other people who could have possibly been on the spectrum due to their personality types, but I would never know for definite.

Dating was a struggle, because of my struggles meeting new people. At school, I was never interested in getting a boyfriend like my peers. They would talk about dating and all I wanted to do was talk about films and my PlayStation. So by the time I was an older teenager, I was already behind in my knowledge of dating and the 'dos' and 'don'ts'.

I had a tendency to fall in love with my best friends. My current partner was one of my best friends for six years before we officially got together and we met in school. I think that the reason I did this was because I felt safe around my close friends and I was already comfortable being around them. I did not have to go on any awkward dates, they already knew me so I did not have to worry about social cues and I could just be myself. Of course, the negatives were that breaking up was always tougher, because it meant that I would lose both a friend and a partner.

What made things harder was that it was always me that ended up heartbroken. I was never the one to do the breaking up, people always left me. Over the years I developed the negative thought pattern that everyone I cared for was just going to up and leave, so I stopped actively looking for a relationship and just carried on with my life, expecting nothing. I shut myself down and became extremely introvert, focusing on my special interests instead. I did want to be with someone, but I was worried I would get hurt. So I did not look and, over time, I became very lonely.

I tried internet dating after I broke up with my first boyfriend. It was ideal because I could chat to someone before I met them in person. This helped with the social anxiety and I could meet them in my own time. I did meet someone but, once again, it did not work out, mainly due to my confidence issues. Had I known I had Asperger's at the time of all of my previous relationships, I am sure that many of my issues could have been improved, if not avoided altogether as proven in my current relationship. It was obvious that I was struggling, but I just could not pinpoint the reasons why. Neither could my partners, it seems.

Looking back I can see my traits clear as day when it came to my relationships. Dating another Aspie for me had its perks. For one thing, we both had the same interests and would obsessively talk about them for hours on a day-to-day basis. I was at college when I was with my Aspie boyfriend which worked out well, as we thought in very similar ways in terms of our college work. When our brains came together, academically, we were the best in our group and both maintained focus when trying to finish an assignment.

The downside for me of dating another Aspie is that I found the other hard work to deal with sometimes. When I was having a bad day, chances were, they were having one too and we became very disconnected from each other. We could not comfort each other either because we were both focusing on ourselves. We also could not read each other's body language so we often misunderstood one another and took comments too personally which caused bickering. When I am having a day where my mood is low, I become extra sensitive to things that are said and, because I had put my own personal defences up, I became very blunt. So we went around in circles and both upset the other through blunt comments.

It was good in the sense that we enjoyed each other's company. We both had no real interest in making other friends because we found other people hard work and exhausting to be around. While this was a good thing at the time, if you then go through a break-up, it is hard to find people to turn to because you have isolated yourself a little.

My personal view is that an Aspie/PNT relationship can be as equally rewarding as an Aspie/Aspie relationship, as long as you have an understanding PNT. I have found that my relationship with my current partner has been far more fulfilling because he keeps me grounded. He is very calm so when I am upset about something, so I calm down quicker because I can see the difference between him and myself in that moment. It helps that when I am panicking about something, he understands what I need at the time. He knows that I will come to him if I need tactile affection when I am upset and that sometimes I do not want to talk about it until I am ready.

The main negative I have is the same problem I had in the Aspie/Aspie relationship; I cannot read the other person. This is the main cause of an escalating meltdown because I will misinterpret signals from my other half and think he is thinking something he was not. In an argument, I can easily mistake a calm expression as meaning that he does not care. The next thing I know, I am upset and crying and he has not got any understanding of what had just happened. Suddenly he was in the wrong and had no idea why. I cannot express my feelings, so when I try to put into words how I am feeling or why something has upset me, it makes no sense to the other person. I have either left them very confused or I have left them thinking that I am not actually that upset. It can be very frustrating, especially when it is the latter.

When I feel insecure, I can often pester my boyfriend for reassurance that everything is OK. Not just once every now and again, but several times throughout the course of the day. While he has never complained, I am sure that this is probably quite tedious and frustrating for him. I cannot stop myself from asking, I just need that extra reassurance when I worry. This is also something I do with friendships too and it has often driven my friends away.

On the upside, I would say that I make a relationship very playful and light-hearted because I am quite childish and silly when messing around. I am not afraid to just be myself and enjoy things that a PNT might miss because of my childlike mind. This means that we can have a lot of fun and laugh all of the time. He has often said that he likes that I was quirky and interesting. I would imagine it is because I do not follow the same social rules and live my life how I want to, not how others want me to. He also does not mind when I obsessively talk about my interests, as we have a lot in common, so that has helped too.

It all comes down to a good understanding of each other. Every relationship is individual to the people in it. I do think there are definitely times when being the Aspie in the relationship has caused issues where a PNT would not, but then I think Aspies bring something different and exciting to the relationship that maybe a PNT would not. Every relationship has its positives and negatives but, as long as the two individuals understand and respect each other and have a laugh along the way, they should all balance out nicely.

Chapter 16

Finding Out That the Two of Us Share a Place on the Spectrum

C.A. Smart

Introduction by Dean Worton

It is interesting to learn of two people both with unknown Asperger syndrome (AS) meeting on a regular dating website. I guarantee that this is not the only case. I do think that people with AS tend to gravitate towards each other due to similarities and connecting with each other in a way that might never happen with a PNT, so when two partners suddenly realise that both are autistic it's doubtful that it's coincidental.

In so many cases, people with autism who have not had the best relationships with the PNT majority have found happiness and solidarity with someone they share a place on the spectrum with.

The interests that C.A. Smart shares with her husband seem quite autism-friendly and I imagine shared with quite a lot of autistic individuals: travel, theatre, live music, cats, sci-fi, cinema and eating out. Sci-fi can often feed the AS imagination and I own a small AS forum where everyone seems to love cats.

My husband Nigel and I met in 2007, through Match.com, a regular dating website. Neither of us knew we had Asperger syndrome until after we had married and moved to our own place.

My Asperger syndrome manifests in social awkwardness and in taking things very literally. I do not understand sarcasm and take everything at face value. I was bookish at school, and could never understand the need for small talk. I usually had one close friend, and could not understand why I didn't have more.

I take comfort in knowing that I have Asperger's because it helps to know that I am not strange. I researched the syndrome after seeing a woman with Asperger's in the Nordic crime drama, *The Bridge*, and have subsequently been diagnosed. Saga, the protagonist, sniffed her armpits and changed her clothes in the workplace, both of which I also used to do in full public view. She was blunt like me, and had to ask questions to understand what was going on socially. Saga was incredulous, like me, that her colleagues took a coffee break and, when she tried to join in, she really put her foot in it and it was a disaster.

Nigel has not sought a diagnosis because he does not want to be labelled, however he recognises himself when reading about Asperger's. He also doesn't want to let his parents know in case they blame themselves for not accepting him the way he turned out. Nigel is a train enthusiast. He builds intricate train sets, is organised, stores and keeps everything down to his first pay slip from 25 years ago and has been perfectly content on his own. He did not have any intimate relationships before meeting me. He enjoyed being alone. He is a meticulous planner and finds unscheduled changes difficult to cope with. He finds working in and with the public stressful, and needs downtime.

I was diagnosed with paranoid schizophrenia at age 17 and I'm now 40 years old. I have switched medications several times, and have now found a medication that keeps me well long term. I have been close to being relationship addicted in the past and I have gone from one partner to another from age 15. I was promiscuous from time to time, in line with my diagnosis of schizophrenia. I have been celibate for short periods, when my interest in Buddhism began, although I have less interest in this now. I still go on yoga and meditation retreats occasionally. I was periodically highly sexual. There was a string of short relationships and some long-term ones where I was not able to feel any affection through anything other than sex. I found intimacy through sex very easy, and kept everything else at arm's length. I always reacted to close contact sexually and was incapable of normal hugs.

I have my sanity, which would not really be possible with another man. I have never come close to being able to live with someone of the opposite sex, being quite terrified of the prospect. When moving in with people I have twice found myself much closer to a psychotic break. It may even have been the tipping point from which psychotic breakdowns have started. I have attempted to move in with two men and some kind of hell followed both times.

The first time I was obsessed with whether or not I liked the man. This was to the point where I finished the relationship just to stop my head from buzzing with the question. After we were finished I thought, 'Well, yes, he was a lovely man' and I did like him. This was a bit too late.

The second time was with an abusive boyfriend, my first long-term relationship. This man was quite a nasty piece of work. I was with him because he pushed all the right buttons for me, the buttons that I had always wanted pressing. I think if these extreme and long-term episodes of my schizophrenia had not happened within this relationship and that my mother had not been able to intervene in real fear for my life, I would have stayed with him until he had no further use of me.

I believe that with this particular previous relationship, I have found out the invaluable – that abuse is actually damaging and is not the best thing for me. I really did need to know this within a relationship. I needed to find out that it hurt me as a person and that it hurt my functioning. Without this I still would have wanted my husband to treat me badly on some level.

We each have at least one good friend outside our marriage. We both have an interest in the outdoors, travel, theatre, gardening, live music, cats, sci-fi, cinema and eating out. We are really happy. We share an interest in food generally, and I cook most of the time. I have started going to a drama group with the aim of performing. I have also, in the last two years, started writing for theatre.

I have found love and safety with my husband in a way which I would never have thought possible. Because we are both on the spectrum I believe we have an enormous capacity to understand each other and to be patient with one another. We both have a very silly sense of humour. We are both kind to a fault. We both do everything possible not to cause harm (although I can lash out to those I am close to), a basic trait we share. We accept our differences and not want to change anything about each other. We have the personal space that we need to be comfortable in our own skin. We have a close friendship.

Chapter 17

Welcome to Planet PJ

PJ Hughes

Introduction by Dean Worton

It is very common among those on the spectrum to only want a relationship if it happens organically. I suppose that on balance people with Asperger Syndrome (AS) have enough challenges in life without adding another that might not feel necessary for survival (except of the human race). Working full time as PJ does can be exhausting as it is for some people with AS. I can relate!

There are often things that traditionally (though not always) the male is expected to do for the female. Many females of course do make allowances, but hopefully one day there will be even more, especially if increased autism awareness comes into play.

A note about touching on first dates: some males on the spectrum are unaware of boundaries around this. However, some form of light touch is often expected by a female date such as a fleeting light touch on the arm, hand or shoulder. Most women won't turn down a second date due to the absence of a hug or kiss if one of these alternatives is used during the date, but don't panic if you don't have the nerve to make physical contact. Just go with the flow and enjoy yourself.

My name is PJ Hughes and I was diagnosed with Asperger syndrome in 1999. And, yes, PJ is my real first name. While I was given a different name as a baby, I changed it to PJ after I was diagnosed and as a result of the diagnosis. Initially PJ was a nickname obtained while at polytechnic, as it then was. Now, my old name, as far as I am concerned, is a term of abuse.

I have never really had a partner or romantic relationship as such. I am not really looking for one either: it's more a case of if it happens, it happens. There have been one or two situations that could be considered as coming close, but not a proper relationship as such. The problem is I found the ladies really demanding: I want this, I want that, etc., but very little coming in my direction. I often got the impression that they wanted me to sort out issues they had where they could have easily sorted it out themselves. While I generally don't mind helping if it's appropriate, they seemed to be too reliant and needy. Once, maybe twice, this may be a way to 'get started', but when it happens often, that becomes a different issue with me. I know any relationship is a two-way thing and I do make an effort, but going through is more a hindrance than a positive way of living! Although I do think this may be part of the flirtation process and if things like this happen too much then it becomes a waste of time for me.

In many ways, I much prefer being single as it is very much less hassle. It may be more expensive and things do not get done as quickly. Unfortunately, this also makes time very tight at times, particularly since I rely on public transport. It has fewer problems associated with it. Being in a relationship is not a priority for me for these type of reasons. Maybe the hobbies I have may have been geared up to minimise this happening. For example, I am a film fan and this wouldn't be conducive for entering or being in a relationship or, certainly, the windows for this would be quite small. Additionally, I think previous and other negative experiences with people definitely would not have helped in this. Being single means it is easier for me to do what I want, when I want, etc. This is naturally dependent on things like living within my means and my activity being legal! As far as I am concerned, there is nothing wrong with being single and not worrying about looking for a partner.

No doubt there are downsides such as not having someone to confide in, share experiences with and so forth, but these can also be done with friends. While for all intents and purposes having friends is useful and important, I think it will ultimately come down to how close they are before a sense of discomfort kicks in and knowing how best to communicate with each other.

If I found myself in a relationship, I am sure that I would have to try and get used to getting into a different routine structure that would very probably change on a regular basis. This would, I argue, be a form of teamwork and learning to work together for long periods of time would have to be developed. Doing this at work can be done, but I go home afterwards. This is different and there would be no 'escape factor'. I would hope any partner would understand and I would try and understand her. Good, understanding communication would be an underlying feature.

I wonder if my sense of humour gets the better of me in the initial process and can put the ladies off after a certain period of time. I also suspect that I find it difficult to spot whether she's interested in me and this being shown through non-verbal means. Similarly, I probably get myself misunderstood because I find myself fancying a nice lady and then my mouth starts working at a speed faster than my brain can manage. I am sure that I am not the only one who has done this. I am very probably not the first and, no doubt, not the last! One thing I do make sure is *not* to touch (specific areas especially. A shoulder may just about be okay depending how it's argued, but other areas, certainly not!).

That would definitely be taken the wrong way and could be illegal!

I do genuinely believe that there is a major problem with being expected to fit in even though it is perfectly normal (for me) to be alone. I am certain that I am not alone on this. And, to be honest, it is often much more interesting! I don't intend this in an offensive way; I guess it is just the way it is. I totally understand that there will be those who will disagree with me and each to their own. I think there is an ingrained pressure to have sexual relations as well.

Generally, I do feel there is a pressure to achieve various 'milestones' within the assorted timescales. I don't think it may always be intentional, but the sensations do come over! For example, there is a sense of 'duty', so to speak, to have sex and, in time, perhaps marry (I know this is not as true nowadays) and have children, etc. And I think this is a problem. Simply because there are far too many human beings on this planet and attitudes like this don't help. I would argue that all this fits in to a certain conformation of society.

Sometimes I wonder whether having a diagnosis would affect my feelings in searching for a partner. And to what level my understanding plays a part as well. I think this would certainly be probable. Trying to reminisce over four decades of living, it would be difficult to remember everything. I have definitely made friends, lost them and found some of them again through the likes of Facebook. I suspect that the then undiagnosed Asperger syndrome of my youth and university study (pedantically polytechnic at the time) would have had an effect of making friends and, where relevant, taking this to the romantic level. I know there was certainly one, maybe two, fellow students I fancied, but never manifested. I think there may have been certainly one that showed interest in me, but I could never quite work out how to 'follow the relevant path'. In some ways, I am probably flirtatious but I am open as to whether it is a serious attempt at developing a relationship or not. I guess this is done, in 'Asperger syndrome terms', with a knowing and cheeky glint in my eye!

Now that I have been diagnosed, I do think to myself that any girlfriend wouldn't have English as a first language. The irony of this is that, apart from watching films, I do like learning foreign languages (French, Italian and Spanish). In a way, I believe that this could be a good way of talking to people, although the way of doing it can be worked out as and when, such as e-mails, face to face, ringing each other and so forth.

The more I have thought about it, the more I have felt that being yourself and listening to your own feelings is important. I feel that one shouldn't worry about not having a partner just because other people are in relationships. If it happens, it happens; if it doesn't, it doesn't. I think the main problem lies in the (perceived) pressures and social norms. The more I have considered the autism spectrum, the more I feel that I am an individual with my own interests. If it does happen, I do think that a mutual understanding is useful and to be able to recognise, for example when I need to be alone or when I need to have a meltdown without having to fully justify myself, etc. or the equivalent for any partner. There will be various things that I do that any potential partner may find difficult, certainly at first. I think it is things like routines, liking to be by myself a lot. I have lived alone for some 15 years and I have become very used to it! Living with someone again will take a while for me to get used to; having said that, I like to think that I am the type of person who tries to reach a middle ground in situations like this. Thus, if the partnership is worth keeping, then something would get sorted out!

As I have noted, I generally find it easier to be alone and, as such, having a partner can be difficult particularly since I have got used to this way of life. However, I would argue (or, indeed, suggest) for anyone who has a partner on the autism spectrum developing a good general understanding of the subject and then unlearning it to some extent. This is simply because it is a very individual condition. Routines, etc. usually exist for a reason and deviating from them can cause a very negative reaction. So, learning to live and work with the condition is important. This is the philosophy I go by! I would also suggest that communication and patience are also important especially if your partner doesn't readily (and naturally) tune into other people. Trying to communicate is something I would also suggest to the autistic side as well, or, certainly, giving it a try. Trying to work together, trying to understand each other, etc., as well as accepting each other's foibles. This is probably obvious, although there will no doubt be exceptions! It's not necessarily about making suggestions, but communicating and understanding.

Chapter 18

Will I Get It Right Next Time?

Philip Bricher

Introduction by Dean Worton

Why oh why can't people just be true to themselves and be proud of others who are? I've yet to work out the mystery of why so many predominant neurotypicals (PNTs) play games instead of telling the truth. Because of this tragic aspect of human nature, a younger Philip lied to people who might well have been lying themselves all to save face. It's odd that people with Asperger syndrome (AS) feel somehow less socially able than people without and yet the people without it often have to make stuff up to fit in socially. So Philip found himself doing the same. If only schoolchildren with AS knew the strange mind games that PNT schoolchildren play, and sadly the same in adulthood. The fact that everyone seems to treat love and sex as a game, and not be straightforward is very sad.

It's only human nature to flirt and 'playing hard to get' or teasing a potential partner in another way is all part of it, but in society in general I think that it can get out of hand, so where someone on the autistic spectrum comes into play, such confusing behaviour is likely to be a recipe for disaster. That said, I guess that some unintentional confusing behaviour from people with AS could in some cases be misread as flirtation. To the untrained eye it could appear quite comical at times, and in some ways this is one of the wonderful things about autism, and might pay off in some cases, but all too often being the AS individual on the receiving end is not funny at all.

I write mainly as one who has perennially struggled with relationships. I was teased about girlfriends at school, and perhaps in youth groups of sorts (and possibly by family members), when at that time I really had no interest in that sort of relationship, and with some Christian teachings of sorts I have more recently heard, it seems rather unreasonable that they were trying to 'sexualise' me before time!

Then in sixth form and early university, I was generally not ready for a girlfriend, but tended to lie about having one, seeing that it seemed unheard of or shameful not to have a girlfriend (if you were a boy! And vice versa would probably be true too!). I was generally a shy, reserved, private person, dedicated to my studies, and didn't like people to know too much about me, although, in my first year at university, I started to spill the beans on a few home truths – another being even my diagnosis of AS! Also, a flatmate at that time helped me to see that not having a girlfriend wasn't such a matter of stigma as I had expected. That lifted a bit of a weight off my shoulders, and I learnt to accept (at least temporarily!) that it is not 'uncool' to be single!

Prior to my second year, when my social life was still quite minimal, and I was still quite dependent upon my family, I spent some of the summer recess at a day centre elsewhere in Northamptonshire, and a young woman there seemed to take a shine to me. I was very naïve about it, and assumed that, because she liked me, it was impolite not to reciprocate. In a way, I did enjoy the closeness with her on trips we went on as part of a group, but there were some ways in which I figured things might not bode so well. Also my family and a Christian brother helped me see that it was not the crux of a healthy relationship in a way – she had the little-known condition, Cohen's syndrome, and despite having all but a decade on me, was very childlike in her ways, and lacked independence and things (even though her head knowledge on certain matters was quite commendable, and more commensurate with her age!). It is a regret that I let it go on as long as I did, people said I was effectively leading her up the garden path, but I was still under the illusion that having any form of girlfriend would put me in a better social standing than having none. However, my second year at university began with a bang – everything happened at once, and I was taken aback by the change in workload compared to the first year. As the months of stress and hard work wore on, I found the idea of having a 'girlfriend' of sorts so far away (at a time when I could barely handle public transport!) untenable, and I nearly broke down with stress with the pressure going on around me. As a result, I took measures to cut one of my modules and, when the dust settled, I found there were a number of girls to whom I took a shine, which struck home how unhappy I would be to stick with the young woman I knew from the day centre. The fact that these said girls possibly didn't reciprocate was not entirely the issue – it was more that it gave me a wake-up call, alerting me to the fact that I was not totally happy with said woman from the day centre and thus had to do something about it, and thankfully she was due to be spending some time in town that February, some six months after we'd initially met. And I did what seemed the right thing, and tried to establish that I didn't want things to continue further, and indeed felt a release from it. It just seemed that it hadn't really sunken in to her by that point, but nevertheless I felt better for making the effort!

Anyhow, from my mid 20s or so, there has been somewhat more development in the way of finding/developing a relationship. My efforts tend to vacillate between 'hitting on' people I meet in everyday life and ones I have met on dating websites, as well as a small number of events geared up for singles (which have generally seemed fruitless in the long run, partly due to lack of anything suitable within smiting distance of me – as well as the recurrent difficulty of knowing how to react/break into conversation/etc.!). I will hereby concentrate the next few paragraphs on a discussion of my experiences here.

Regarding the former context, in many cases I have naïvely assumed they'd be more interested than they are! I might meet a girl in a social setting, feel a connection or attraction to her, and wonder how to take it forward. This tends to be coloured by being in some doubt as to when, where or how often we are likely to meet in the future. I have had moments of having feelings for girls I might meet in a temporary setting, which would seem strong at the time but, once I return to normality, the feelings all but fade into nothing! Perhaps this goes to show or reinforce how the 'butterflies in stomach' that can be experienced in the nascent stages of a relationship is prone to fade away when the dust settles – and the old joke is that in a relationship, 'how are you?' becomes 'where are you?'.

Conversely, there can be an opposite danger of sorts of forming a relationship with someone in a close setting such as a common place of work or worship, whereby it would become awkward if the relationship fails and both parties still have to face seeing each other in their new lease of life as 'singletons'! Generally, I either do nothing (out of uncertainty as to how to take it forward) and tend to fantasise about it, or make my views all too obvious, and risk coming on too strong. It has been a challenge (and work in progress) to know what signals to look out for – giving either extreme of response! However, sad to say, they are often indirect with me, and say that which they think I want to hear (normally an affirmative in response to a proposal to meet for a coffee or something), which gets my hopes up, then the next thing I know, I end up being treated as *persona non grata* – usually in the context of a blocking on Facebook, and I will be left perplexed as to why things took a sudden nosedive after picking up what seemed like good momentum! I would often attribute it to a bad run of luck, or down to insecurity or change of heart on their part, but would struggle to know at what point I might have made a faux pas!

From time to time, it has been fed back to me (possibly with good reason?) how I have been known to be familiar/affectionate with young ladies in various social settings, such as church or orchestra rehearsal. Unfortunately for me, out of seeming respect for privacy of the individual(s) concerned, I am often told that it 'doesn't matter' who was involved or what was the exact context, but then it means I cannot associate it with signals beforehand or evaluate any potential damage as a result – irrespective of whether it seems fitting to approach (not confront!) said individual(s) myself – which deprives me of the learning opportunity, never mind the assurance that any specific case(s) may have been resolved! In any case, the reason for my acting that way in the first place, far from being a pervert, may have been a mixture of desire or intention to be friendly towards them and potentially pitching it wrong, as seeing to tackle loneliness and desire for affection within myself. In fact the former of these has raw memories when, at a church where I formerly worshipped, I used to complain when next to no one would speak to me after the service over refreshments, but yet when I sought to make a new female student feel welcome and included, it evidently misfired, and my efforts seemed to spur her to change churches!

Anyhow, the main thing I wish to achieve in writing this is to encourage people to be more upfront to us about their emotions, not just giving a 'green light' response artificially, but also making it clear when (or perhaps how!) the listener needs to back off, hopefully in a way that would preserve the friendship as it is! (However, of course the occasional genuine 'green light' would be very much desirable!). Well, it may not help preserve a present friendship/acquaintanceship, but if it provides lessons as to how to deal with a future scenario, then it is still useful! In any case, a lesson I am partly learning from this is putting out feelers – as if to be 200 per cent certain that a person means what they say when they give that which sounds like an affirmation! For instance, when I recently met a female friend socially – a friend who was engaged to be married – as if to avoid the pitfall, I asked how her partner would feel about it, and she said that he wouldn't mind, as she has lots of male friends. And I'm glad to say that it was successful from that angle! However, I am aware that the issues of meeting a spoken-for woman one to one can be a grey area, and this requires much thought and planning.

There is a certain amount to say about the latter context (i.e. online dating), but in a way it seems to take a lot of trawling through several profiles on a site, finding people with whom I feel a connection, and, for those who reply, it may not be obvious how to prolong the contact – which may mean much of a commonality is not present! However, in a small but substantial number of cases, it has led to a stream of messages, which has sometimes led to other media of communication: e-mail, Facebook or mobile text messaging – which sometimes stand the test of time and even to personal meeting – although during the period of writing (2014–15), it has often been the personal meeting that seems to have let things down, as of seven of such cases, only one I have seen a subsequent time (even though I didn't envisage a relationship developing out of it, and I gather neither did she), and with one of the others there has been sparse contact since. However, in a rather upsetting way, the third case led to no further communication whatsoever – which seemed a blow seeing that I felt a strong connection with her, and especially enjoyed her company! Still, it seems one of life's bitter lessons to learn, but then there may be other cases in the pipeline.

With two of the later ones, when we met there was a mutual feeling of incompatibility (in one of those cases, neither of us saw the need to follow it up afterwards)! With one of the two remaining cases, I had an unrequited interest in one of them – but at least amenable contact followed; and in the final case, with a small-built East European girl, we seemed to get on really well, but it was unclear what path we should take. Indeed, this was confounded by the perennial issue of a long-distance relationship – in fact none of the above-described were in my county of Northamptonshire. Some of them were in neighbouring counties such as Warwickshire, Bedfordshire or Oxfordshire, but others were as far as London or the South Coast! – but it presents the difficulty of whether we could see each other often enough, and for long enough at a time – as well as the critical question of whether one or other would be prepared to up sticks and move – something I contemplated in two previous relationships, as to be described below! However, a main factor against my following up with this most recent date, aside of losing her phone number due to having mobile phone problems – was because a relationship started to form with a girl who started coming to my church (wherein I also deactivated my profile on the site in question)! The start and end of this recent relationship has been a new occurrence, since the original submission of this manuscript, but I shall proceed to unpack the nuances of that later on.

In fact my two most serious relationships (of sorts!) were one each of these methods and, as intimated at the close of the last section, a much more recent one since the commencement of writing followed the manner of the former method, that is, 'hitting on' people I meet in everyday life. Neither of them lasted more than a couple of months

– at least without some sort of interruption, in the case of the first one, where she got cold feet twice before deciding to break up with me proper! Oddly, the first two cases were confounded by the presence of a second interest in me – and in both cases both the girlfriend (of sorts) and the 'rival' effectively went by the wayside at the same time – and not necessarily from finding out about their competition!

The third and latest case was somewhat different – she suspected that something of that sort was going on (at a time when I was physically below par, and under pressure about things), but in reality she had misinterpreted something I said (albeit with gratuitous zeal!), and jumped to conclusions in her own hasty zeal, without allowing for a proper discussion! Much as I consider myself culpable in part for its demise, nevertheless, in the scheme of things, I think this was merely the straw that broke the camel's back seeing that the last month of the relationship was rather tempestuous between us, and she and her family, whilst as good as accepting me among them, seemed to have unrealistic expectations of me, which rather than encouraging me to do better, actually served to make me feel inadequate! Additionally, she was nearly ten years my junior, and much less independent than me – she still lived with her parents, and hardly went out of their sight (and for instance, she first went out of town without them only during our relationship!). It had a few striking resemblances to the case with the young woman at the day centre described much earlier in the run of things! She might have been desirous for the company and affection of a relationship, but seemed to lack certain life skills about it, as might have I in some ways! Indeed, it was a bit of a shock to me for someone to suddenly be expecting commitment after a prolonged period of being single and having tried various means to meet a partner! However, this could well in part have been an outward manifestation to issues under the surface as to areas of incompatibility we both naïvely seemed to overlook, and were barely willing to discuss, or able so to do without there being confrontation!

Ironically, whilst the relationship was still going strong, her father had occasion to lend me a book about 'How to do almost everything' – which included a section about relationships. Whilst not my initial interest in the book, I was naturally drawn to this section if only to give a health check to the relationship! It explained, among other things, how to know that a relationship has run its course, and how to go about ending it. However, regrettably, the way things happened for us was not the recommended way in the book – along the lines of being open and upfront about it, as well as choosing a sensible moment. However, in her case, she seemingly assumed that the prolonged silence would convey the hint to me! It would have seemed healthier if she had found a way to express how my words or actions had hurt her in the way they had, rather than storing them up and using as a weapon against me! However, I have to be careful to accept my own share in the blame, without holding myself accountable – or allowing others to hold me accountable – for that which lay outside my hands! Still, after the break-up, despite the struggling to adjust to the change in circumstances and relation to her family, etc., hopefully there is material that can be learnt on both sides!

Now, looking back to the earlier two cases. The earliest of such cases was when a well-meaning university friend was trying to set me up with her college friend, not knowing of the relationship I was already pursuing, which to all intents, didn't appear totally secure at the time, and curiosity got the better of me. The build-up with the 'second girl' in that case seemed promising, but once we met in person – in a stressful setting – things quickly turned sour, and to this day I am blocked from/by her on Facebook (barring a window when it seemed things were more peaceable between us!).

The middle case was when a girl with whom I had been indirectly connected for a while declared an interest in me.

In the early days of my knowing her she was already in a relationship and was trying to set me up with one of her best friends, which interestingly was fruitful in so much that she actually became one of my best friends too! Anyhow, the relationship with the girl (who was trying to set me up!) was short lived and very much compromised by the fact that after a period of intense work (and thus not having time to meet, even though she gave mixed signals about that!), she was preparing to move to Devon to further her study, and as soon as she started to get cold feet, a second girl came out of the wings! And it goes on, that things with the second girl picked up just as things with the first girl rekindled, and things went through phases of being on brilliant terms with one and at loggerheads with the other, and I was confused by the whole situation, and unsure of the best move to make, seeing that it seemed not a mere question of tossing a coin for me to decide! I could not accept the idea that *neither* girl might be right for me – it seemed unthinkable that this could have been anything other than my 'epiphany' with relationships – but indeed that was how it went! The most painful thing, almost as with the experience a couple of years earlier, was that both 'possibilities' ran dry around the same time (in the most recent case, when the 'rival' found an albeit short-lived boyfriend), which seemed to affect my mental/emotional and physical health – especially profoundly the second time around!

I was in a bad way for months, and it seemed weird to let go of various plans to meet the more promising of those girls at various future instances, e.g. half-term and Christmas, as well as realising that the idea of getting a place together in the future was suddenly a non-issue. And at least in the near future thereafter, such things as seeing couples around town holding hands, or hearing about people going away 'with their partner', as well as hearing cheesy lines from pop songs, reinforced the pain for me (in a way that has thankfully much subsided since!). It had been as if I were having to rewrite my life – that I'd been on holiday from the real world for while, and I was struggling to settle back in! I guess there were reasons why I found it hard to accept such a number of problems at the same time, and in my stress and disappointment, I was running various friends dry in my quest for consolation.

It seemed I was so doing in a couple of different ways – partly that things left me grief-stricken, and I needed to let that out of my system to them; but also that they probably expected me to learn more than I actually did or could on their first telling. Therefore I would have lots of questions, checking that they had correctly understood a scenario, and investigating whether various nuances would make a difference. This however, seemed to come across as 'rejecting their advice', which was far from my intention, and an awkward case of getting wires crossed! Their well-meaning advice to 'move on' seemed meaningless, however.

I did even consult my GP seeking counselling, but merely to be told that there was a long waiting list and that they weren't that specialised in such conditions as autism anyhow! Also, in the days when the relationship scenario was still rosy, things went haywire with the support I was receiving, and that took a couple of months for any replacement to materialise, and even that took months further to build up proper rapport once had it started. However, perhaps unsurprisingly, the recent case was rather easier than the first two, seeing that the circumstances of the break-up were a little different, as well as having had the previous experience, etc. (Plus the fact that I went on a holiday of sorts just before the impending break-up gave me some valued time away from the problem, even though it was not a pleasant thought coming back to it!)

Anyhow, to bring the reader back to the present, time has in many ways been a great healer, as things develop and occurrences become more distant, although (as anticipated!) it has proven a long painful way up, and not without other fallouts on the way! Still, there have been various things for which to be thankful, including musical pursuits/achievements, various trips and even new friendships that have developed, some of which have helped keep me in the strai(gh)t and narrow! Also I would refer the reader back to my words surmising the importance of direct communication about the recipients' emotions, keeping the Aspies' learning in mind as much as possible, as well as (more predictably!) the comfort of the recipient! That way, the Aspie should learn to adapt to the neurotypical world as much as possible, as well as their own flaws and ways of thinking becoming more widely accepted!

Chapter 19

'Doing Social'

Don't Talk <u>At</u>, Talk <u>To</u>

David Smith

Introduction by Dean Worton

The first couple of pages of David's story could just as easily have been written by a predominant neurotypical (PNT) individual but if you read enough between the lines you can see the Asperger syndrome (AS) undertones. He mentions having had several relationships over the years. To some, it might sound impossible for this to happen to someone on the autistic spectrum, but it comes in so many different shapes and sizes. It's not always about the numbers, it can also be about the relationships themselves.

David sounds like he can manage socially whenever certain factors come into play, possibly learnt behaviour. This has undoubtedly helped him to form his relationships but of course the relationships themselves have often been full of challenges. Not that relationships aren't challenging anyway, but add AS into the mix and the challenges can turn into a real minefield. However, David has had some good relationship experiences too. So, like with so many other things, relationships are still worth working at for people with AS even if it takes more work or more time.

When I was a child of around three or four, my older sisters would be press-ganged into taking me with them when they visited their friends. My sisters hated this, of course, because I was *a bit of a handful* and it usually meant that they would either have to cut their visits short or content themselves with playing outdoors where the effects of my behaviour were less devastating. It was through my sisters that I made my first 'friend', Johnny, who was the younger brother of their friends, Rosie and Anna.

I don't remember much about the first couple of years of my relationship with Johnny, but between the ages of five and seven I'm sure he was the only significant friend I had. I think the majority of the time we played together was spent jumping over a strange, rusty crossbar affair they had embedded in the concrete at the top of some very steep steps that led up to their front door, or jumping from the roofs of a couple of nearby air-raid shelters that the local council kept neglecting to demolish. That's what I did, anyway. I'm not sure what Johnny did, but as long as he was somewhere within visible range I was generally content to consider that we were playing together, and my sisters were content to consider me *babysat*.

I remember that another boy, Robertino, would sometimes play with us, and that generally Johnny seemed far happier when he was around than when it was just the two of us. I can also remember losing my temper with Robertino one day and jumping on his head while Johnny cheered me on. I may have been fighting Johnny's battles for him – I was fiercely loyal when he was slighted in any way or when he asked me outright to defend his honour. I never really questioned that, because to me it was simple: he said he was my friend and you stick up for your friends. I used to fight my brother Stephen's battles for him too, despite the fact that he was three and a half years older than me and that outside of these brotherly interludes we usually fought like cat and dog. Of course his enemies were three years older than me too, which speaks volumes about that aforementioned sense of loyalty as well as highlighting a marked lack of awareness regarding self-preservation.

Johnny's family moved away when I was seven, and I don't really remember having any friends for the next few years save for a strange girl called Georgina who everybody else ignored. I played with (alongside?) lots of kids at school, equally happy to join in with the boys playing football or the girls skipping and twoballing at the opposite end of the playground. But these were casual acquaintances rather than the solid friendships other children seemed to be forming. I can remember being curious about this, and wondering particularly why adults seemed to prefer my generally hateful brother's company over mine, but I wasn't lonely or upset, just confused. Years later, of course, I realised that while he was often spiteful and self-serving my brother also had charm, while I, straightforward and honest to a fault, was pretty much charmless. I don't think the hyperactivity helped either, or my vile temper when I believed myself the victim of some injustice.

After primary school things went a bit pear-shaped. I had peritonitis at 11, followed shortly afterwards by what was effectively a nervous breakdown believed at the time to be some form of post-traumatic stress disorder (PTSD). I walked out of secondary school at 12 and didn't go back. I did keep up a fairly casual 'alternative' education at a special unit for kids who, for one reason or another, were not coping in mainstream schools. But the reasons for me being there were misunderstood so it was more a case of 'warehousing' than a differentiated education.[1] I did successfully maintain

---

1   This would have been around 1972/3, so the psychiatric team involved with me would possibly have had some limited knowledge of 'Classic' Kanner's autism, but none whatsoever of high-functioning autism (HFA) and/or Asperger syndrome. While my underlying difficulties were recognised and recorded they were attributed more to my dysfunctional home life and to vaguely defined psychiatric disorders arising from medical trauma.

a few relationships with equally oddball friends, but these did not extend beyond the school gates and disintegrated after I stopped attending at 15.

Between my 16th and 17th birthdays I had a couple of epiphany moments. The first of these was when I realised that I was not the repulsive, mentally retarded, psychopath (sorry if that sounds offensive to anyone – it's just representative of some of the milder insults being constantly thrown at me at the time) my family had led me to believe and the second was when I identified the single most important factor that would contribute to my future wellbeing, my life was going to be shit if I didn't do something about it.

The first of those life-changing realisations was a huge shock, and to this day I sometimes have trouble convincing myself of the truth of it, despite all of the evidence. The self-loathing I felt for myself between the ages of 12 and 16 is still very much part of who I am and can still force its way behind the psychological driving seat. I tend to swing between this and a level of (probably) unjustified arrogance which can annoy the hell out of those who don't get to see the whole picture. The truth is somewhere in the middle, I tend to be very good at the things I'm good at but absolute rubbish at everything else. It's not a case of being 'average' or even competent at the *everything else* (which probably accounts for my chequered employment history), it's a level of dumb incomprehension which even I find baffling, so must be doubly so for those who've never encountered it before.

The second realisation was simultaneously terrifying and liberating. Having spent the largest part of the past four or five years lying in bed reading books or listening to music (I emerged only to eat, or, when I wasn't 'resting' between sackings, to go to work) I forced myself to grasp the nettle and create some sort of social life for myself.

My first foray into wider society was with a boy I knew from the council estate I'd recently moved away from. He was visiting his older brother who had just moved into a flat near my mum's, and when we bumped into each other he suggested we go out for a beer. I'm not quite sure why he offered or why I accepted, we had never been friends before and to say he was a nasty piece of work would be a massive understatement. He was the second youngest of six or seven nasty pieces of work, and I think that his position in the pecking order imbued him with an additional degree of cunning that provided an extra dimension to the kind of mindless thuggery enacted by his older brothers. I suspect he asked me purely so I could supply him with free beer, and I accepted because I was basically too stunned to do otherwise. There was also undoubtedly an element of *beggars can't be choosers* to my acceptance of his offer: I was desperate for friendship and under such circumstances even Hobson's choice can seem attractive.

I met him and his girlfriend in a pub in the centre of town, and over the course of the evening I discovered for the first time the delights of alcohol. After a single pint of lager I thought it wasn't really my thing, so switched to Bacardi rum, which tasted fine if you topped it up with coke. I have no idea how many times I 'topped up', but I became vaguely aware after a couple that I suddenly felt very erudite and witty and that all my nervousness had evaporated. After a few more I went from being erudite and witty to being *loud*, and from there to being incoherent and insensible, but by this time I was oblivious to the progression. I was ill for three days (I have never drunk Bacardi since) with what I suspect came dangerously close to alcoholic poisoning, but I did learn two valuable lessons: alcohol makes talking easier, and girls like boys who can make them laugh.

A few days after I was fully recovered I was surprised to get a phone call from the boy's girlfriend; they had split up, and she wondered if I'd like to take her out one evening. If I'm totally honest, she wasn't really my type, but at that time I was too inexperienced to know that I had a 'type' so gratefully took her up on the offer, after clearing it first (that honesty coming to the fore again) with the boyfriend to confirm he was truly no longer interested. We went out twice, having awful sex on the second date (awful for me because I hadn't a clue what I was doing, and awful for her because she didn't have a clue why I hadn't a clue what I was doing but was too polite to say) and 'splitting up' the following day. The night after that the ex-boyfriend found an excuse to beat me up. I'm sure it didn't have anything to do with the girl herself, but on a psychological level for him it did have something to do with 'ownership' of the *Oi, are you looking at my ex-bird* variety. Ever practical, I figured taking one beating was preferable to taking several, which would have been the natural outcome had I fought back and attracted the attention of his older brothers, so I just lay back and thought of England while he pummelled away. I can remember laughing at one point but that just seemed to enrage him further so I kept quiet after that apart from the occasional 'ouch'.

While my relationship with the girl failed, my relationship with alcohol went from strength to strength. Thankfully, I'm not a person with a predisposition for alcohol or drug dependence, otherwise my reliance on alcohol as a social crutch could have been really problematic. Between Thursday and Sunday night I could take it (and take it I did!), but I could quite happily ignore it for the rest of the week and return to my mild mannered non-drinking persona of bedroom music and literature guru.

For my first few outings into the big wide world I tagged along with my older brothers – probably the only time that being the youngest of seven has worked to my advantage – but after a while I had a small group of friends who I felt confident enough to go out on my own with. This was the first time as an adult that I ever felt accepted within a group of people of my own age, and when I realised that they actually *liked* rather than tolerated me the change in my personality was swift and dramatic. I remember one of my brother's girlfriends saying to me at the time that she found it hard to believe the 'cocky little sod' (she meant this affectionately, I think) in front of her was the same person who used to sneak off home after silently downing a couple of shandies just a month or so earlier.

Hyperactive by nature, I could 'play' the life and soul of the party brilliantly, and was extremely popular with the small group of people I kept close to me, but the extremes of my behaviour were always a double-edged sword. I had a definite role within my social group as the ice-breaker and joker, but my unpredictability made the same friends nervous if I tried to step outside of that role. It also reinforced the barrier I was placing between myself and wider social interaction – people liked me, but they didn't 'get' me, and that made them wary. While enjoying my newfound popularity I was also very aware that the mask I wore socially was only one facet of a far more complicated whole, and it always stung that by and large the 'whole' was not what people wanted.

With the benefit of hindsight it's easy to see that I must have had something going for me at 17. Though I didn't know it then I was actually quite good looking – not a 'ten' but certainly a six-and-a-half/seven and possibly an eight on a good day – and when my confidence was high (bolstered by drinks and the company of friends I knew and trusted) I could be funny, interesting and smart. My fascination with wordplay and for jokes actually worked to my advantage in 'chat-up' situations (I think the wordplay is just the way my mind works and the jokes arise from that and overcompensation for not being able to understand them when I was young. My brain just automatically stores every joke I hear for the purposes of cross reference), but would let me down in the one-on-one scenarios that followed. I had no intuition at all about when and how to move from jokey chat to more serious courtship, and became awkward and tongue-tied when the initiative was taken for me. I was incredibly naïve, and girls that did like me had to be pretty obvious about it before I would realise and respond. Looking back I can see there were many, many lost opportunities, but suspect I'm still as slow on the uptake with new situations that might develop for me.

Just before my 17th birthday I had my second sexual encounter, after being 'seduced' by an ex-work colleague 12 years my senior. It's every 17-year-old near-virgin's fantasy, I'm sure, to have a lovely more mature woman assisting his rite of passage, but in my case it proved an unmitigated disaster. I was too scared to admit my inexperience and she was too embarrassed by the whole situation to 'take me in hand'. So I was out for a duck twice, and beginning to wonder whether this whole relationships thing was actually worth the candle.

My first *real* relationship began around a year later, a month or so before I turned 18. I kept bumping into a pretty blonde at a nightclub I went to, but it took me a while to realise that she always seemed to be floating around. Eventually we got talking outside of the club at a taxi rank, and I offered to share my taxi home. I was shocked when she told me she lived in the same block of flats as me and regularly said hello when we passed on the stairs. I think that away from my friends I was so self-conscious I never actually looked up. I was aware that there was a pretty young blonde living on the ground floor, but had never recognised that pretty blonde as the same one I saw at the nightclub or as the person who said hello to me on the stairs. It turned out she had had a crush on me for months after seeing me tinkering with my motorbike under her bedroom window, and had effectively been ambushing me every time she saw me coming. We started dating almost immediately, and were a couple for the next three years.

The relationship was not a particularly happy one. Jenny was a bit odd herself and neither of us was very good at compromising. She was an only child and her mum and dad were a bit odd too – her father was an incredibly gifted electrical engineer who should, by rights, have been making a fortune as a chief designer for the Ministry of Defence or somebody, but instead struggled from job to job as a self-employed electrician. In its own way Jenny's background was as dysfunctional as my own, and with no other models to aspire to we both thought our turbulent and destructive relationship normal. Nine times out of ten if we went out together for the evening (or even shopping) we would end up walking home on opposite sides of the street, sulking or shouting abuse at each other over the tops of passing traffic. Between rounds we were a very loyal, loving and caring couple, but as time went on the impossibility of the situation was becoming obvious to both of us.

We finally split up while on a year's working holiday in Australia. Jenny was doing well as a waitress at the local hotel in the almost exclusively male mining town we lived in while I was struggling to hold down increasingly crappy part-time jobs. In the end I decided to come home and she decided to stay. I think she had an Australian guy waiting in the wings because she married and moved to Perth just a few months later, when her visa was due to run out. I was quite relieved, but it took me a couple of months to realise it. I also realised that relationships like that were destructive, and made a vow to myself that I wouldn't make the same mistake again.

Since breaking up with Jenny almost 30 years ago I have been in many relationships, the shortest lasting just days while the longest spanned more than 11 years – the first nine some of the happiest of my life, while the last two nearly killed me. Sometimes even good relationships end badly, and that's a risk you have to take. Investing in a relationship that starts badly is something to be avoided. I wish I'd known that 30 years ago. I hope I know it now.

I guess relationships are a bit like giving up smoking – success should be measured by how few times you've been through the process rather than by how many. *Giving up smoking is easy – I've done it hundreds of times* is hardly a recommendation for the position of mentor, is it? Similarly, if someone claims to have had many *failed* relationships it could be taken as a good indication that you're looking in the wrong place for any reliable sort of advice. But I don't think it is. Because when I look at the lives of people around me – autistic or neurotypical – getting relationships *wrong* seems to be the rule rather than the exception.

What is a relationship, anyway? And who makes the rules about how they work? I have a relationship with my cat – I feed her, pay all her vet's bills and stroke her when she fancies it and she periodically tries to trip me up while I'm carrying sharp implements. On the surface it sounds really destructive, but in reality it's probably one of the most stress-free relationships I've had, and – as any cat owner will attest – if she wasn't equally happy with the arrangement she would have buggered off years ago. Compared to my relationship with my son (who for the record is the best thing that ever happened in my life and the reason for the 'some' inserted in the earlier paragraph about the first nine years of my longest relationship) it's a doddle!

Some couples seem to need to live in each other's pockets, while others start to feel claustrophobic once the initial 'rush' dies down. Both styles seem to work perfectly well when the couples are 'in balance' (comedian Peter Cook lived in a completely different house 100 yards up the road from his third wife during their marriage and said he thought it would be the preferred choice for many if they could afford to do it), so it really seems to come down to personal psychology and preference; one man's meat, and all that...

I think other questions that are particularly relevant for autistic people are what do they want from a relationship and why do they want it? Is it about 'fitting in', or does the desire for a relationship arise from internal need? Social contact for people on the spectrum can be hugely stressful and emotionally draining, and external judgements and expectations about their relationships can compound that stress. Personally, I've found since my diagnosis that I feel far more empowered to say 'no thanks' to social contact I don't want, but I can equally see that I might have made choices if diagnosed at 17 that would ultimately have been disempowering. If I hadn't felt the need to 'play the game' I would have missed out on milestones and memories in my life that I now cherish, but I only have the emotional frame of reference to recognise that with hindsight. I believe that's what they call a *Catch 22*.

Stuff I've got wrong

Sadly, no matter how much you might protest that you *don't do social* (to quote Sigourney Weaver in *Snow Cake*) the chances are that there are going to be times when *social does you*. With that in mind, I thought I could offer some observations on things I've got wrong over the years. I'm not sure I'm qualified in any way to tell people how to *do*, but I do have bags of experience on how not to do:

- I'm really lucky that my 'special interests' are socially acceptable special interests – music and books (I think if I'd had access to the technology during my formative years I'd have probably been a 'puter nerd too, which seems to hover in a sort of dodgy 'up to a point' grey area in general society these days). That said, what I failed to realise when I first forced myself out of my social comfort zone was that while most people *like* books and music their relationship with those things isn't the same as mine. It took me a long, long time to learn that people – especially girls in night clubs – didn't generally want to discuss my album collection or swap book titles in a cosy little reading-group-for-two in the corner. Quite often I could see their eyes glazing over, and I did make the connection between that and them disappearing to 'the toilets' and never coming back (*I'm leaving now. I may be gone some time...*), but I just didn't really have much else to offer, and when I panicked it would only make the situation worse. Whatever your special interest is, join a club (or an internet forum if you want to take it slowly) dedicated to that. You stand much more chance of coming into contact with people who do share that special interest, and having that resource as an outlet will hopefully help you to avoid the topic in situations where it's going to hinder you rather than help. I surprised myself when writing this, because I realised that none of the people I have had significant relationships with have been particular 'musos' or readers. They listened to music and allowed me space to listen to mine, and some of them were occasional holiday readers, but not one was the type to have two or three books at a time on the go or to spend hours sifting through racks of sale CDs in HMV. It seems odd, seeing it in black and white that things I have always considered so important to me haven't been significant to those I've loved and who have loved me. Another thing that's just struck me: they didn't have *anything* that they were that passionate about. How *odd!*

- Don't depend on alcohol as a social crutch. It can be your friend, but it's a bit two-faced and can turn on you. Drink slowly, too, because if you drink fast it can take you from behind. From eloquent raconteur to staggering tosspot takes far less time than you can imagine, and when you arrive at the first point the chances are you've already booked your ticket for a junction further up the track.

- Humour, like alcohol, is a beast with two heads.
  If you're lucky enough to be able to 'do' funny it'll
  open all sorts of doors, but you need to be sure they
  are doors you want to open and you want to be sure
  they're not just leading to convenient 'boxes'. It *is* true
  that girls like men who make them laugh (and men
  like girls who make them laugh – but not too much as
  it gets a bit competitive), but they don't tend to take
  them *seriously*. Give girls a choice between Johnny
  Vegas and Johnny Depp as a dinner date and they
  might have to think about it. Ask them which one they
  would rather have a breakfast date with and it's odds
  on Vegas won't have to share his full English.

Never try to impress people with how clever you are, even
on your 'special interest' subject. I used to try to show people
how clever I am, and in reality it was dangerous territory,
because I'm nowhere near as clever as I like to think I am.

- Being interesting isn't about showing people
  how much you know, which can seem pushy and
  intimidating, but sharing your thoughts and opinions
  with equal consideration for the opinions of others.
  Nobody loves a smartarse.

- I don't have too many problems with making eye
  contact but I know my body language can be 'off' and
  I'm aware of some other traits and mannerisms that
  can be a bit off-putting. Try to maintain eye contact
  (or look as though you are – without staring – God it's
  complicated isn't it!) even with people who know you
  have autism and who accept and understand that it
  is difficult for you. The same applies to other body
  language (mirroring, etc.) if you can. Yes, it is totally
  unfair and totally wrong and it should be 'okay' not
  to have to put yourself through it, but the reality is
  that these signals *are* part of communication for most

people, and on a subconscious level it will make a difference to how relaxed they feel communicating with you. Probably the big thing to remember is that you are doing it for *you*, not them, it is a means to an end. Most autistic people I know do, when feeling relaxed enough, make some eye contact unconsciously with people close to them. Doing it consciously, outside of that comfort zone, is purely a device to get you to that 'relaxed' point.

- Sitting on stairs at parties looking miserable in the hope that someone will take pity on you and talk *never* works. People go to parties to have fun, not to cheer up miserable sods. Besides, 'pity' isn't a good basis for any sort of conversation or friendship anyway, and you're more likely to attract someone who *likes* that dynamic rather than someone who wants to help you change it.

- Relationships are a two-way street. Try not to invest in ones that are one sided, and don't expect others to invest in you on that basis.

- Relationships should be fulfilling. Don't feel pressured to 'conform' and seek relationships just because it's the done thing. Maintaining relationships that make you unhappy more than they make you happy is pointless and destructive. Sometimes breaking away from them hurts terribly in the short term but has long-term benefits.

- Relationships can hurt. Pain is a worthwhile emotion too.

- People will often not live up to expectations. They have that right – they are not *their* expectations. Try not to measure what other people do by what you would do, because they will often disappoint. I tend to be very loyal and trusting, and for years assumed that other people were like me in that respect. The hurt I felt on discovering that my assumptions were wrong would have been diminished if I hadn't been so sure of my convictions at the outset. Trusting people is one thing, but you have to offer trust on the understanding that it *might* be betrayed, and that the risks involved are worth it. Lying falls into the same category. I'm not much of a liar, but to assume categorically that others don't lie is asking for trouble. By the same token, if you're a habitual liar, don't project that onto others and mistrust them. Give them the benefit of the doubt until you have good reason to think otherwise. If you're really lucky, they'll never give you good reason, which has got to be a bonus in anyone's life.

- Try not to be too intense. Intensity can be scary, especially for new friends. Try to listen, too. Talkers can be entertaining but listeners make us feel wanted and appreciated. If I'm relaxed I can be a fairly good listener and give people the space they want and need. If I'm stressed or socially uneasy I tend to dominate conversations or fall silent, and instead of listening I often find I'm just rehearsing my next speech in my head or planning my escape. Most of the time I forget, but if I *can* apply the mental brakes to slow down and listen, the conversation will be more fulfilling for both of us.

Finally, an interesting observation made by a friend of mine... Most (but not all) of the people I've had relationships with have been a bit 'quirky' themselves, or have come from backgrounds where one or both significant role models (mum and/or dad) has been a bit 'quirky'. I wouldn't go so far as to say that any were undiagnosed autistics, but there were certainly traits floating about at above average concentrations. Chances are they didn't notice the things that I got 'wrong' or judge them quite so harshly, purely and simply because they were things they could recognise and accommodate quite readily. By the same token, I wouldn't judge unusual traits in them that maybe would have made other men wary. That sort of unconscious acceptance would have been reassuring for both of us, and with stress levels greatly reduced we would have been able to function more appropriately anyway. That's one hell of a positive cycle, but does sort of predict that people I develop relationships with are going to be as 'quirky' as me in some respects. I'm not sure if that's reassuring and positive or something to worry about, because in a Venn sort of way the things we overlap on are likely to be positive for us, but when we clash the chances are we're going to clash big time. Or perhaps that's how it is for everyone? Because, as I said earlier, getting relationships right seems to be the exception rather than the rule.

Chapter 20

Happily Married on the Spectrum

Paul and Elizabeth Wady

Introduction by Dean Worton

It is wonderful that Paul and Elizabeth have a relationship in which they do everything together. They have both found solidarity in their shared diagnosis of Asperger syndrome (AS). Both are considered different by society in general and both are presumably misunderstood by many, but they both have a mutual understanding of why the other is the way that they are. For example, most people wouldn't understand about the stim words, or at least not most predominant neurotypical (PNT) individuals, but they can appreciate these things about each other and escape into a world that might not make sense to others but to them means everything. It's easy to tell that they are soulmates.

PAUL: I was diagnosed December 2004, during a court case in the Bristol Magistrates Court in which my best friend from junior school and I were acquitted of common assault. The courts paid for my diagnosis. I had no idea I had it. I was 41.

I met Elizabeth in a London social group February 2005, and we began our relationship April 2006, three months after I commenced work at head office of the National Autistic

Society. I've been a permanent member of staff ever since. I spent three years teaching Buddhist meditation in the Acton service, travel the UK doing corporate training in autism which I now write, and set up and ran the Ladbroke Grove centre adults' social night before moving to the Brokerage Department, formerly Person Centred Planning.

I filmed and voiced the Ask Autism training module films, with a script by my friend Dr Dinah Murray, and now have the book *Guerilla Aspies* out.[1] I've got a show for it too which I'm taking to the Edinburgh Fringe this year. Isn't attention deficit hyperactivity disorder (ADHD) a wonderful thing? I even make music too, at The Model Aircraft Museum. Every song about autism. My ambition in life is to sit still.

Everything in my life is based around my marriage, and means nothing without Elizabeth's presence in my life.

We married within two years of starting our relationship in December 2007, when we were both at the age of 43. It is really not long enough. We understand each other perfectly and share a private space that may be a bit beyond my describing. We have the same innate nature, characteristics and behaviours and even share stim words which we repeat to each other all the time.

We have many friends and family who are on the spectrum, such as my father and Elizabeth's late one. We find it difficult to find Aspies we can relate to. Most of us in the position we are in tend to hide and mind their own business. Or never even heard of autism I'd imagine? Diagnosis tends to come when things go wrong.

We have always maintained we had nothing to say about our life together because it was all so straightforward? What can I write? I do my stuff and Elizabeth has her own private room and space to do hers? I have the living room because I love having her around all the time? I could be writing or composing and she's just sitting in the corner, reading away

---

1   Wady, P. (2014) *Guerilla Aspies: The Guerilla Aspies Handbook*. Rhos on Sea: Dark Windows Press for Free Autistic Press.

as usual? We have our favourite TV shows such as *NCIS* and *Grimm*, and I subject her to *Dr Who* as a matter of course. I started with the DWAS (Doctor Who Appreciation Society) in the 1980s and saw the first doctor episodes, or so my parents told me.

ELIZABETH: After reading a small section in the *New Scientist* magazine in 2003 I realised that the symptoms attributed therein to Albert Einstein and Isaac Newton were exhibited by my father, my grandfather and myself. Nine months later on 17 March 2003 I was officially diagnosed as having Asperger syndrome. My age at the time was 40.

In February 2005 I went to my first social group for those on the spectrum, not feeling the need to do this until then. Very quickly, after about 10 to 15 minutes, someone poked his head over my right shoulder whilst I was speaking to another person. This was Paul, my future husband and, yes, our relationship is still as unusual as our first meeting. As an example, later that evening, Paul wanted to take a photograph of me so I screwed up every feature on my face to make it appear 'funny'. Paul tells me that was the moment for him, as he then realised I was not just a science teacher but as eccentric as he was!!!!!

We are different people but in many ways the same, something I would imagine is true for all individuals in a successful relationship. We both do silly things at home (no, I am not going to reveal what these are), we like walking and watching factual programmes on television. Additionally, we are both able to understand what the other feels and thinks with or without explanation.

Paul does things spontaneously, which I detest as I am a forward planner. He also has a habit of wanting me to do something when I am busy doing something else, this is annoying. However, neither of us can always have their own way so we have to compromise. In our marriage service we promised to love each other in sickness, in health, whether we are rich or poor until death parts us, this, amongst other things, means compromise. I have at least managed to get him watching detective stories, all those dead bodies, wonderful!!!!!! (fictional ones). I am thankful that Paul also tolerates Pushkin, the cat, leaving hairs around the house and letting him sleep on our bed in winter. A man who likes animals is definitely one worth having.

As a couple we are happy in each other's company but also regard it as normal to do separate activities, he goes to his room and creates music on his machines and I read books. Being together sometimes and apart at others means we are less likely to get on each other's nerves than we would if we were always together. Although we married late in life and so far it has only been seven years I look forward to another 10, 20, 30 or more years together.

Chapter 21

Anniversary Flowers
It's the Thought That Counts

Jules

Introduction by Dean Worton

This revelation that comes about only as a result of the childrens' diagnosis could actually have saved thousands of marriages. Statistics would be interesting.

Asperger syndrome (AS) and unwritten rules are not a great match as the individual in question does not always innately 'know' what the done thing is in a given situation and actually needs telling. As a person with the condition myself, I've learnt some of these rules from books and been surprised in some cases, that a particular thing even was 'a thing'.

The flowers from Jules's husband for whatever reason, very likely related to his own autism, were not presented in a romantic way, but in his mind he got his wife a present to show how much he loved her, and they came from him, which is what is important. I would urge all predominant neurotypical (PNT) readers to always appreciate their AS partners for all efforts they make to show their own appreciation.

We were 14 when we first met and this year those digits will be reversed. That feels like a long time to know a person and yet I wonder if I do really 'know' my husband. I think he might be an Aspie and if he is I have misunderstood him for 25 years...

Four of our children have Asperger syndrome. I have had to learn all about what this means for them and to adapt my parenting to meet their needs. This newly developed understanding of autism led me to wonder if my husband too could be an Aspie (and my father and my brother!). It would explain so much – about him and us and our relationship – and about why I was drawn to him in the first place. It turns out that, without my knowing it, many of the important/influential men in my life are probably autistic – Aspie is my 'norm'.

It took two years for him to first communicate with me – having been in my maths class all that time – and he did it by writing a message in Tippex on my bag, 'you smell' – not the most romantic of starts.

He was commonly understood to be 'hard to know'. He had a long-term 'best friend' who was popular and gave him access to the 'gang' but he was always on the periphery – not disliked but different – certainly not like the other boys who were into sport, bragging about sexual conquests and generally arsing about. He was more like me – had teachers for parents, enjoyed classical music, read literature, didn't quite fit in.

We made friends gradually – walked to chemistry together, sat together in the common room, went out of school together to buy lunch. I could talk to him about 'stuff'. I gossiped and he listened. He got to know people through me without actually having to interact or do the small talk – I was sociable enough for both of us. I enjoyed his company and gave up an A level to share 'free periods' with him. I liked being 'the one' – chosen by the boy no one really knew – I felt special (and as a girl with confidence issues I needed that). He had an older girlfriend who had already gone to university and I had other boyfriends – each of whom would eventually give me an ultimatum – they were jealous of my 'special' friendship. I always chose him.

So we grew up together. My parents were miserable – my dad was mentally ill (treated for over 20 years with a vast array of antidepressant and anti-anxiety medications in combination with sleeping pills – all of which he abused – in an attempt to get some respite from feelings that were probably the result of being autistic and not knowing it – he was 'burnt out' by 47 and had retired on health grounds) so I escaped home and ate tea at his house every night.

We did our homework together, he taught me to drink and to smoke, stayed by my side at parties, danced all night with me at the Ritzy and made me laugh. He was beautiful and clever and funny and he liked me – I was drawn to him and felt 'connected' – he seemed familiar and felt comfortable. We watched the same films over and over and these, along with Dépêche Mode, The Smiths, New Order and The Stone Roses, became part of our shared world. We did not need to talk much – we were happy to just be.

It did not matter to me that he started drinking a lot – we were only 17 – everybody drank – or that he lied to his parents (about everything). I thought it was cute when he styled himself on the 'bad boy' from our favourite film. He was cool and I loved him – secretly of course – I still had other boyfriends and he had his older woman.

He started to miss school and would drink his parents' alcohol at breakfast. We skipped chemistry lessons and went to the pub – I would catch up the work later but he didn't. If we all went out (our big gang of mates from school) he would be the drunkest, the most wasted, the risk-taker, the law-breaker and the gambler. We warned him he was going too far – he never listened. He gave up his clarinet and classical music in favour of ecstasy and raves. He was fun to be around – everyone liked him but still nobody knew him – he didn't talk or share himself but he played drinking games, cracked jokes, did brilliant impressions and sang. He was fun.

He didn't do well in his A levels – we all spent too much time in the pub but, unlike the rest of us, he seemed unable to factor in revision time or manage his workload. He just carried on regardless – sticking to the same routine no matter what he had on the next day. We went off to different universities and I missed him. We spent the first five weeks of term without contact (mobile phones did not exist) and then he called – on the public phone in my halls of residence. He had split up with his girlfriend and he wanted me. He came down on the next train and that was it – we were 'together' – that was in 1991.

In 1994 I graduated and he didn't. He had never liked his course but did nothing about changing it. He partied all night and slept all day. He failed his exams, then his retakes and was expelled. He told no one – not even me. His parents found out through a letter from the grants office – they were devastated. He refused to go home and moved into my flat. There were no repercussions – not really – for what he had done. The drinking, the smoking the gambling, the pretending and the lies he had told all went unchallenged because he refused to engage or talk about it.

We felt sorry for him (his parents and I) because he seemed so helpless. We were worried about him. We paid off his debts and bailed him out as we always did (there had been many other things over the years and have been even more since). I searched employment pages, wrote applications and helped him prepare for interview. He got the first job he went for and stayed with the same company until he was diagnosed with cancer ten years later. By then we were married with three children. I had married him – despite everything – because I was in love with him, because I couldn't imagine life without him and (if I am completely honest) because I thought he would grow up – I really thought he would change. That was 16 years ago and he hasn't.

Recovery from cancer led to retraining, self-employment and two more children (there was a desire to make the most of life). I soon realised that for my husband's business to succeed I would have to take responsibility for customer contact, make the appointments and manage the finances. It became clear that without predetermined company structure and rules to fall back on, my husband could not organise himself or plan ahead. He could not predict the outcomes of his behaviour or consider its effects on others. He was unable to manage customer expectations or conflicts – and there were plenty of those. He increasingly needed alcohol to reduce his social anxieties and enable him to deal with people face to face (he started drinking on the way to work, and then during the working day, and then just every time the effects of the last drink started to wear off). Self-employment was, in hindsight, a poor career choice.

Now my husband is 'broken'. Physically his back has given out, causing him intolerable pain and preventing him from engaging with most of life. Mentally, years of self-medicating with alcohol to cope with the effects of his anxieties have taken their toll. A year ago our marriage and he were in crisis and he wanted to take his own life. Now, with professional support and his parents' money (again), the crisis is over and he is limping forward – an ex-alcoholic with no job, no ambitions and a brain too addled with pain medications to concentrate or focus on anything but Lego – the return of a childhood obsession. I remain his 'chosen one'. He has no friends or world outside our family.

The problem with being neurotypical is that it is all too easy to see life from one's own perspective and assume others' understandings of situations are shared. But what if they are not? When I discovered my husband's drinking (and all the deceit that had gone with it) I believed it demonstrated that he cared about me so little I couldn't stay married to him. He then demonstrated that he cared about me so much the prospect of us separating led him to attempt suicide.

How can two people have such different understandings of the same relationship? When I get to glimpse the 'core' of him – the man behind the behaviour – I love what I see and I want no one else. I don't want to lose this warm, funny, intelligent, charming man who has shared what feels like my whole life. In the moments when we reconnect I know we will be together forever – it is in the times between – when I feel increasingly isolated and alone – that the doubts creep in.

It's a shame that I only see the 'inner' him when we are at marriage breaking point – when he has no other option left than to share himself. He finally talks – about him – who he is and why he does – and what is going on in his head. I never cease to be astonished by what he describes and he is always astonished that I don't already know. What I glimpse is a lost boy. He reveals confusion and vulnerability and a complete misunderstanding of my point of view. He shows me another perspective that is alien to my natural way of thinking but has its own logic. His hurtful actions are almost always the result not of thoughtlessness but of lack of thought (the distinction here for me is that the first is selfish and uncaring – deliberately disregarding others' needs or feelings – the other stems from something entirely different). His motivations are not what I assume them to be and therefore I need not take offence or feel hurt. It simply does not occur to him to consider the impact of his behaviour on others. He does not recognise and then disregard my feelings – they don't even enter his consciousness.

If I hadn't discovered autism when I did and begun to understand and empathise with autistic thinking, we may not have made it.

We are trying new strategies. We no longer assume that we share the same perspective. We clarify what we mean – I make requests explicit and stop expecting him to follow hints or understand how I am feeling from my behaviour. I tell him how what he is doing is making me feel. I am still upset if he chooses to do it anyway but that's OK – it's open and honest – and he usually doesn't. I piss him off too

– lots. But now he talks me through his thought processes – I explain mine – we share our astonishment at each other, accept each other's point of view and compromise. We are bridging the divide created by lack of intuitive empathy – a concept I am only just beginning to truly understand. It was not because he didn't care about me that he provided no emotional support when my friend died, when my father was sectioned, when I miscarried our baby or when our children were diagnosed – or indeed any of the many times when I desperately needed him to 'be there' and he was anything but. He doesn't feel my pain or know how to react to it. He doesn't have the capacity to know what to give me in times of emotional distress – I now understand that this does not mean he doesn't care.

I understand this but I am not always understanding

It was our wedding anniversary on Friday. He bought me beautiful flowers but he didn't give them to me. They were left in the kitchen sink for me to come down to in the morning. To me a bunch of flowers in the kitchen sink does not *feel* 'romantic'. I think 'anyone can buy flowers and leave them in the sink...I could buy myself flowers'. I want more than just the flowers. I want my anniversary flowers to *feel* special – for him to do or say something that shows how much he loves me. What I want is for them to have some special words attached. I feel ungrateful.

He doesn't get it. It was our anniversary – he remembered – he bought me flowers. How they are presented (or not) is not the important bit for him. He isn't aware that I feel that *his* giving them to me is the *one* thing that *only* he could do and therefore the thing that would make them special to me – different from the ones that come from other people or that I could buy for myself. I was hoping for a 'gesture' and he doesn't do gestures. From his point of view he bought me flowers and I wasn't grateful. He can't win. No matter what he does he gets it wrong. He doesn't understand what I want and so, no matter how hard he tries, I am not satisfied – I always *feel* that there is something missing and that pisses him off.

In writing about 'Anniversary Flowers' I have come to realise that I am still expecting/hoping for something that my husband – the probable Aspie – is not able to give and that is unfair of me. *I* am still hoping that *he* will change – after all these years. But, although he never asks it of me, it is me that must change because I am able to and it is I who wants things to be different. I must *genuinely* accept that what he can and does give is of no less value because of the manner in which it is given. I often think I understand this and determine to accept it – but then I forget again. It's so easy to forget and to go back to viewing everything from one's own perspective – it's like a default setting. At this very moment I understand that I need to stop interpreting his actions as if they are those of someone with a neurologically typical brain and accept, that as a reflection of potentially different thought processes, they hold a different meaning. I hope that I will remember this more often.

My flowers are beautiful. They are the right colour, the right type, they don't include lilies (which I hate), and he chose them himself.

I am going to go downstairs right now and say 'Thank you'.

Chapter 22

Love (and Sex) Is
Just a Game

Gwen Greenwood[1]

Introduction by Dean Worton

Not only does having Asperger syndrome (AS) make dating culture already confusing but Gwen also has to negotiate lesbian dating culture. I imagine that some of the rules are likely to be similar to those for gay men, but there are undoubtedly many differences too. I believe that both gay and lesbian dating culture is more open than heterosexual dating culture and perhaps ultimately it is more accommodating to the AS mindset, though I'm no expert and suspect that as with most experiences ultimately its all very personal depending on the individual. I admire Gwen's openness about her sexuality, as not enough people are open about it. Society sadly is not as accepting as it should be, although it is heading in the right direction nowadays.

Although I agree that preteen relationships do serve a purpose, I'd say that they could be quite hard to come by for AS individuals and many people with AS, especially males, could be between 25 and 35 when their first relationship starts and sometimes a lot older.

---

1 Please note that, while I use my own name, the names of the other people in this story have been altered for their privacy and protection.

'Your Dad just kept on pursuing me, and I liked that. Women like to be pursued because that makes us feel desirable.'

'So…if I ask a girl out and she says no, should I leave her alone or should I keep pursuing her?'

'Well that depends on a lot of things.'

'Like what? For God's sake, I wish people could just be honest about what they want. It would make things so much easier.'

'Well, sex is a game.'

I had this conversation with my Mum a couple of months ago, and while it left me feeling more confused than ever, it also struck a chord with me. Sex is a game, and sometimes it feels like everyone knows the rules but me. Although I'm currently in a relationship and get on very well with my partner, the social rituals involved with dating and sex continue to confuse me.

A lot of neurotypicals assume people with autism have no interest in sex and aspire to be like emotionless robots. This couldn't be further from the truth. I think a lot of people with autism experience such overwhelming emotions that, instead of processing them, we just bury them in our subconsciousness. This can make us seem like emotionless robots. But the emotion is always there, and eventually it will resurface ten times stronger than it was when we chose to submerge it. This aspect of autism can make romantic relationships very confusing, as it means it's hard for us to put the routine fights and disagreements every couple has into perspective. Of course, that's if you reach the stage in a relationship where you know each other well enough to fight. For many years I struggled to make it past the third date.

I'm going to examine my previous relationships and what went wrong, in the hope of proving some insight into the rules of the game.

I started dating when I was 11 and a boy from school (Leon) asked me out. It was one of those freaky, preteen relationships where you try and copy the behaviour you've seen in romantic comedies. When we kissed he used so much tongue it felt like there was an eel wriggling around inside my throat. On our first date Leon took me to the cinema to see *Garfield* and wrote my name on his pencil case. Gradually, we started to lose interest in each other. There's only so much fooling around you can do before you've developed breasts. Plus I was starting to be branded as a social outcast at school, so it wasn't good for Leon to be seen with me. Soon he dumped me for a girl who'd already started puberty; he crossed my name off his pencil case and replaced it with hers.

Now I'm older, I find those kind of preteen relationships really freaky. Kids that age shouldn't be snogging! They should be playing in the sunshine or watching CBBC. However, I think preteen relationships do serve a purpose. They allow you to learn some of the basic rules of dating before you're old enough to get your heart broken or contract a sexually transmitted disease (STD).

So what were the rules I learned from my first boyfriend? First, I learned that the money spent on dates should be split evenly. We were both too young to have much cash, and at that time my mother was a hard core feminist – she would have been furious if I had let him pay for everything! Second, I learned that it's important to have a shared interest to talk about. Thanks to my Asperger's, I tended to do a lot of monologuing about my favourite TV shows instead of the normal back and forth exchange of conversation. That was fine when I was talked about TV we were both interested in (*The Simpsons*), but when I moved on to *Doctor Who* he quickly lost interest. Third, I learned that any gaps in the conversation could be filled with kissing, but no matter how much saliva got exchanged it was inappropriate for me to wipe my mouth with the back of my hand.

Although I soon dated other boys, I struggled at school after breaking up with Leon. I had lost my only ally, and found it very difficult to relate to the rest of the class. I soon decided I preferred books to these bizarre, judgemental preteens who always seemed to be gossiping about me. As I socialised less, my autism became more pronounced and I was a target for bullying. I believe that explains why I didn't date anyone else from school.

I found boyfriends in other places, such as after-school clubs and the group of moody Goths that hung around the Corn Exchange. These relationships all ended very quickly, as they weren't all that challenging for me (the thrill is in the chase, never in the capture). I wasn't that interested in the people I was seeing, and a small part of me felt relieved when things were over, as I didn't have to kiss or touch them anymore. Kissing and touching was something I seemed to do a lot of, but only because there was never anything to talk about and I couldn't bear the awkward silences.

I thought that romantic relationships were a dull experience for everyone. Then, when I was 15 I met the most beautiful woman I had ever seen, and everything changed.

Recently Larry (the boy I dumped when I realised I was having feelings for another girl) has asked me why I dated him in the first place when I was a lesbian. The truth is I honestly wasn't aware of my sexuality. I liked dating boys because that's what my neurotypical peers were doing and I needed to know I was just as desirable as a neurotypical. I remember looking at photographs of celebrity couples when I was about 12, and wishing that I was a man so that I could date one of the women.

Despite the many gay and lesbian friends my parents have, I don't think it occurred to me that I could date another girl without compromising my own femininity. Like many Aspies I learned to socialise through television. At first I copied the words and mannerisms of the Disney Princesses (which only made me a laughing stock) then I looked to American sitcoms for guidance on how to socialise properly. During the 1990s there were no prominent gay sitcom characters that I was aware of. And, of course, to this day there are still no lesbian princesses in Disney films, which explains why I continued to look for Prince Charming long after I started feeling more interested in Princesses.

I do feel a small pang of guilt regarding the boys I dated during my teens. With the benefit of hindsight it would be easy to say that I lead them on and behaved quite cruelly. But I was young. Just like thousands of teenagers out there I had yet to discover my true identity, or my true sexual preference.

Anyway...by the time I was 15 I had found my niche in the social caste system of my school. I was still rejected by the popular kids, and I think they were more than a little afraid of my unusual behaviour. However, there were others like me. Nerds, Emos and even a couple of other students on the autism spectrum had managed to band together in a small social group, which I'll call The Rebels. I loved this group because I wasn't under any pressure to conform to social norms while I was in it. I could just be me.

One day I was hanging out with a few of The Rebels at the back of a church, when Imogen walked over and joined in the conversation. She was in the same school year as me, but her class rarely mingled with mine, so she wasn't aware of how degrading it was to be seen with me. Which was lucky, because she was the most beautiful woman in the world. She had long black braids, thick plump lips that looked like two cherry segments, almond-shaped brown eyes and smooth, coffee-coloured skin. When we first met I felt warmth rushing through me. I knew I had to spend a lot more time with her.

I met up with Imogen a couple of times outside school, and it turned out that we had a lot in common. We both loved the music of Evanescence and the movie *Interview with the Vampire*. Unlike the other people at school, I felt incredibly relaxed around her and could talk for hours without worrying about how I was coming across. We watched *The Queen of the Damned* together, and soon developed a code based on the world of Anne Rice. 'Lestats' were potential boyfriends (which she always had plenty of) while 'Like Claudia' was a euphemism for having your virginity. I was like Claudia, Imogen was not.

I started to understand the depth of my feelings when we hung out with a friend of mine (Alice) who also had a crush on Imogen. When we said goodbye to Imogen after mooching round the shops, Alice said something like 'Oh. Now we're watching her walk away.' It was a perfectly innocent comment, but I suddenly realised that I wasn't just watching her walk away. I was watching her long brown legs, and her round buttocks straining against the material of her tight skirt.

On that night Imogen came round to mine for dinner. We went on Vampire Freaks.net, listened to music and tried to watch another Anne Rice film, but had to switch it off because we couldn't stop talking. On the car ride to Imogen's house I noticed she smelled of cinnamon, and another warm, rich, exotic spice that I couldn't place. I felt like I had found my soulmate. But I didn't have a clue what to do about it.

All the social rules I'd learned so far applied to dating boys…talk about a shared interest, kiss to fill up any gaps in the conversation, let him initiate all physical contact so he doesn't feel emasculated, pretend you like love bites – it's just men's way of marking their territory. How could any of that apply to the beautiful, exotic Imogen? Besides, I was pretty sure she wanted a Lestat, not a Claudia.

Me and Alice discussed our infatuation with Imogen constantly, and I don't think I would ever have found the courage to 'come out' without Alice at my side, sharing the journey with me. At first neither of us said anything to Imogen herself. I brooded over her, wrote lovesick sonnets and rang her mobile every day just to hear her voice. Alice got another boyfriend, despite the fact that she wasn't remotely attracted to boys. I made out with Imogen at several parties. So did Alice. But as much as I enjoyed these kisses I knew they didn't mean anything. Imogen had always been an advocate for Free Love.

Deep down I didn't think me or Alice would ever share our feelings with Imogen. Alice had a boyfriend, and despite all the poetry and diary entries I still didn't know how to put my feelings into words. Besides, Alice and I had been friends for years before we met Imogen. Surely Alice wasn't going to let a pretty girl come between us, right? Wrong. Alison confessed her feelings for Imogen despite knowing about mine, and despite the fact that she was in a relationship with someone else. I watched them holding each other in the cinema and wept silently, grateful that the dim lighting meant no one could see how upset I was.

The next few weeks were a confusing time for me. Imogen and Alice were dating, but Imogen didn't seem particularly committed to the relationship. Once she drew a heart on the pavement in chalk and wrote 'Alice + Imogen' in its centre, then paused for a minute before adding '+ Gwen'. She also continued to sleep with men. I imagine those kind of mixed messages would be confusing enough for a neurotypical to interpret, let alone someone on the autism spectrum.

In the end I just pushed it all to the back of my mind. I'd continue to write soppy, clichéd poems about Imogen and eventually blurt out 'I Love You!' through tears several months later. But for now I had far bigger problems.

Let's look at what I learned through pining after Imogen. First, all's fair in love and war, and it's socially acceptable to go after someone your friend likes. Second, some teenage girls will make out with just about anyone; it doesn't mean they're attracted to them. Third, the majority of communication when it comes to dating and sex is non-verbal. A slight turn of the head, a subtle wink – these things can mean more than a thousand words, but their meaning is virtually impossible for someone with autism to decipher. I also learned that being a lesbian didn't mean compromising my femininity. I could wear my hair long, lace my corset tight and plaster my face with make up. Despite social stereotypes, none of those things were a sign of heterosexuality.

Anyway, let's get back to the bigger issues. I was struggling to complete the work for my GCSEs (and later my A levels), my mother had been diagnosed with a life-threatening form of cancer and I had started to slide into depression. I remember walking through school one day with this sense that everything was slowly crushing me to death, like water grinding a cliff face into fine sand. I stole a scalpel from the art department, and when I cut myself I felt an instant sense of relief. It wasn't long before I graduated to using razor blades and chunky pieces of broken glass to cut deeper. Self-injury is very common on the autism spectrum, and I believe it comes from the stress of trying to navigate a world that was made for neurotypicals, or the guilt associated with having extra support needs. The deeper I cut, the better I felt.

In early October I met the woman who would become my first girlfriend. She was a Greek student called Angelika, who had moved to Bradford to study English at the university. I've come across lots of people on the autism spectrum who end up dating foreigners. I believe this is because someone from a different culture is less familiar with England's social norms, and therefore more tolerant of Aspie quirks. Angelika was a beautiful woman who dressed in corsets, skirts that were comprised of layers and layers of netting and heavy black boots. She had hazel eyes, prominent cheekbones and boobs that defied gravity. She was a couple of years older than me, a heavy drinker and lived in her own flat – which made her seem very cool at the time.

Although we dated for about a year, I never told Imogen about her. I think a part of me was hoping Imogen might still change her mind and decide she wanted to be with me after all.

Angelika and I soon settled into a comfortable routine. We'd meet up once during the week for a date, and again at the weekend with a couple of my friends. Sometimes I stayed the night, and although I didn't sleep much in her tiny single bed it felt good to have her near me. We both loved symphonic metal music, solitude, art and poetry, so we always had something to talk about. For Christmas she did two beautiful paintings for me. One featured a majestic, bright green 'spirit of the forest'. The other painting was of two lovers; naked from the waist up in a location she called 'Suicide Lake'. The lover that looked like me was slitting the throat of the lover that looked like her. However, in the end Angelika would be the one to end things with me.

The passion faded after the first few months. We did lots of kissing and groped each other over our clothes, but I was still self-harming regularly, so getting undressed in front of her (a necessary prelude to sex) just wasn't an option. Angelika was very patient with me. She'd had sex with lots of girls before, but she didn't seem to mind that I wasn't ready and never once bought up the issue or tried to force me. Once, she took off my shirt and discovered the scalpel scratches that covered my stomach. As you can imagine, that quickly killed the mood. Angelika solemnly promised that she would 'be strong' for me, but she could barely be strong for herself.

At the end of the year Angelika told me that she had failed her exams and was moving back to Greece. I stormed out of her flat in a flood of tears, just as angry with her for failing the course as I was with her for leaving the country. She'd spent all year telling me how easy it was and how well she was doing; now we were going to have to split up because she'd spent too much time drinking instead of studying! Aspies tend to view things in black and white, and I was no exception. I'd gone from thinking of her as a blessed angel to thinking of her as a heartless devil in the space of a few seconds flat.

I saw Angelika on the night before she left for Greece. Unfortunately she'd booked a hair appointment that lasted several hours on that night, despite having arranged to meet me first. I sat in her flat for hours waiting, staring at her half-packed suitcase and trying to pluck up the courage to flush her passport down the toilet so she'd have to stay. Eventually Angelika returned with blue highlights in her hair and we went out for our last meal together.

That night almost felt like one of our first dates. We talked, ate pasta, made out feverishly and then talked some more. It was surprisingly easy to forget that she would be leaving the country the next day. Eventually, however, we walked back to her flat and I ordered a taxi home so Angelika could pack. When it arrived we both stared at each other helplessly, knowing that we ought to say a tearful, romantic speech like the kind found in girly films but not really having the right words. Then a crowd of drunk arseholes showed up and demanded to borrow Angelika's lighter, completely oblivious to our emotional distress.

The taxi driver got tired of waiting and disappeared along with the crowd of drunks. At the time I was annoyed with the taxi man for driving off, but I can see now that I had no reason to be. This wasn't a rom com. He wasn't going to listen to our tearful declarations of love and clap slowly. He had plenty more passengers to pick up. We said goodbye, I walked down to the bus station and I never saw Angelika again. She had promised to write to me, but she never did, and I lost her address when my wallet disappeared.

So what did I learn from this relationship? Was I any closer to understanding the complex rules that govern romance and sex? Not really. I learned that self-harm scars are a huge turn off, but despite how horny I was that didn't stop me from cutting. I learned that you shouldn't date someone you have too much in common with. Although shared interests seemed like a good thing in the early stages of the relationship, Angelika and I were both introverted and melancholic, and we only intensified these traits in one another. I loved her, but I needed someone who would encourage me to socialise more, not someone who would agree heartily when I said how much I hated humans and offer me gin at eleven o'clock in the morning. She needed someone who would encourage her to socialise more, eat proper meals and seek medical help for her mental health issues. I'd like to think I could take on that role now, but when I knew her I was far too young and vulnerable.

I didn't date for the next few years. My mental health deteriorated and with it my social skills. I continued to self-harm, which meant that sex wasn't an option as I sometimes had open wounds on my arms, legs and stomach. My relationship with Angelika should have acted as a reminder that I had the potential to be an attractive, desirable partner. But the fact that she just left without a trace really unsettled me. I'd lost the camera that contained all her photos, my parents hadn't met her before she moved to Greece and she never wrote to me. At times I wondered if Angelika has been a hallucination. At times, that seemed the only plausible explanation for a freak like me having a girlfriend.

I went back to pining for girls who were way out of my league (and often straight!), writing cheesy sonnets about them but rarely declaring my feelings or attempting to date them because I did not consider myself worthy.

I did go on a couple of dates with a short, pink-haired girl from the Lesbian, Gay, Bisexual and Transgender (LGBT) Society during my second year of uni. After holding hands and passionately making out with me several times, she told me she'd only ever seen me as a friend. I also dated a beautiful blonde with caramel coloured skin after graduating. After holding hands and passionately making out with me several times, she also told me she'd only ever seen me as a friend. These situations left me terribly confused. But they also taught me the most important rule of the game: verbal communication is just as important as physical communication. When dating, you must ask how your partner feels about you and where they are in the relationship. Just because someone seems prepared to have sex with you doesn't mean they actually like you.

For the past couple of years I've been receiving treatment for my mental illness and focused on improving my self-esteem. I've also managed to stop cutting, and most of my scars have faded to pale silver lines that are only visible close up. I no longer feel ashamed of my Asperger syndrome. I think it's a beautiful thing, as it means I experience the world with far more intensity than others. This unusual perspective is what makes me creative and gives me the inspiration to write.

I recently met up with a friend of a friend (Jasmine) for coffee and she commented that it was great to see me with a smile on my face. I looked at her properly. She had pale, creamy skin completely free of make up, short blonde hair and hazel eyes. She seemed honest, kind and she wasn't bothered by my autism. Perhaps I was ready to start dating again. A few days later I met up with Jasmine for a drink. She revealed that she liked me, and after she had driven me home we shared our first kiss. A week later, in the cubicle of a pub toilet, I had sex for the first time and didn't even worry what she'd think of my scars.

Most of the social conventions involved in sex and relationships continue to baffle me. But that's OK. So far Jasmine has been very supportive and understanding regarding my autism. She speaks her mind instead of expecting me to be able to interpret her body language and facial expression. She's honest about what she wants from me, both emotionally and in bed. But she hasn't tried to rush me or make me do anything I feel uncomfortable with. When we're around other people and I don't understand sarcasm, banter or social cues Jasmine corrects me. But there's no sense of malice or superiority – she's simply helping me navigate the neurotypical world.

It's early days yet, but I feel Jasmine and I work well as a couple, and the main reason for that is that we're complete opposites! She's encouraging me to let my hair down and socialise more. I'm encouraging her to go to poetry nights, museums and galleries. Sometimes it's hard. Socialising has always drained a lot of energy from me, and if I'm planning on spending a few hours with her and her mates I generally need to stay at home the next day so I can recharge and be my moody, introverted self. But I have a really good feeling about this.

I don't know what the future holds. I don't know if Jasmine will turn out to be the love of my life or just another girl I've dated. But I do know I am good enough and I am beautiful enough to be in a relationship. I've finally got my mental health under control, and I've never been happier.

Chapter 23

Relationships

Sublime or Ridiculous?

Atul Movelis

Introduction by Dean Worton

I really enjoyed reading Atul's account of his childhood attempts at forming relationships with other children with some unusual yet quite creative and interesting strategies whether they always worked or not. The 'perching' on a corner table in a place of social gathering before anyone else entered was quite clever. It's so strange to think that in the world of predominant neurotypicals (PNTs) it just seems to work, but people with autism often need to look for strategies just to have friends, and indeed even friends can be time consuming for people with autism who most likely need some time alone. As such, relationships are something else all together.

I certainly second the notion that something is ridiculous if done just because others do it that way, for example, shaking hands, an extravagant wedding, asking how someone's weekend was and many more examples. Not that you shouldn't if you want to, but such things should not be automatically expected to happen. We are all individuals.

I rather like Atul's notion of being socially and emotionally ambivalent with most people but then forming deep connections with a chosen few. Many people with autism have a preference for being on their own and it is wonderful when one special person comes along unexpectedly and the person with autism then wants to spend all or most of their time with that person, because they just get them. They make allowances for all the quirks, which generally speaking seems to be part of the attraction. It makes the person with autism unique, interesting and worth getting to know. Thank goodness that some people appreciate autistic people.

I was listening to the radio not so long ago and there was a 'phone in' about what it is like to be in a relationship with someone with autism. I was appalled, alarmed and angry. I even ran to my phone to ring the show and alert them to the ridiculousness of their topic before I remembered that I hate using the phone and am usually pretty rubbish on it without the opportunity to rehearse the conversation several times beforehand, and decided to vent my spleen internally rather than on national radio. I spent several minutes enjoying a virtual phone call instead – not quite as good as the real thing, but a good substitute nonetheless. As it was an imaginary phone call, and the imagination used was my own, I recall that I was utterly brilliant, and in a few scathing sentences brought the presenter of the programme to his virtual knees, while acknowledging my intellectual prowess and irrefutable arguments. Essentially, I pointed out that it was hugely offensive to make a show out of people declaring what it is like to be in a relationship with someone with autism, as obviously each person with autism is an individual in their own right, so to group us all together would be nonsensical in the extreme. In my imaginary diatribe I pointed out that the radio would surely be the recipient of a multitude of complaints had they offered a show on 'what is it like to be married to someone from an ethnic minority', for example.

It seemed to me to be as pointless a subject as simply asking, 'what is it like to be married – full stop'.

Then I find myself writing a chapter on a book about autism and relationships. Strange world, eh?

I don't know what it's like not to be autistic. Bear with me – this is important. I can't guess – or work out – what relationships for non-autistic people are like, so in a sense I don't really know how different or otherwise I am compared to the majority of people. I do know that, in hindsight, after hours, days, weeks – and, yes, sometimes years – of introspection and rumination, I have come to the realisation that social relationships for me have perhaps not been as conventional as I once might have thought. Actually, this is somewhat misleading, as for the majority of my life I never really thought much about my own situation, I simply accepted things as they were and got on with it. It's only more recently, after talking to others (autistic and non-autistic) that I have understood that my assumptions about certain relationships were decidedly misguided. My long term naïveté astonishes me, and yet continues to this day – when will I ever learn! So, here are some exemplars of social interactions that I deemed at the time (and for several years after) as perfectly ordinary and not worthy of considering as 'different' in any way.

My first friend

I remember in primary school 'befriending' the first person I met, a chap who I was told to sit next to in class. In my eyes he was 'available' – as in he was in close proximity to me, and was, therefore, fair game to bestow my friendship onto. I didn't actually know what to say to him, so didn't say anything at all, but simply insisted that I hold his hand. Perhaps understandably (at least to me now) he wasn't at all keen, and refused to hold hands. Such was the distress I felt in this overt and frankly astonishing (to me) rejection I took the only recourse I could think of and retaliated by stabbing him in the chest with a pencil. In hindsight, I am guessing that this is not the best way to make friends.

Interactions at school playtimes

I had no concept of friends, nor how to play with others, but this didn't worry me (at first); as a younger pupil I spent most of my playtimes being the school 'policeman' – a self-appointed role I quite enjoyed. Effectively, I walked around the playground telling people off for either real or imagined breaking of rules. Quite what the other pupils thought of this, I have no idea; their reactions did not permeate my consciousness, so I am afraid I cannot elucidate any further – but retrospectively, I think I may have come across as a little odd.

As a result of my lack of ability to actually talk to anyone, I would buy sweets (Refreshers, as it happens) and come into school early; I would hide these in the desks of people I particularly liked the look of, with the rather questionable rationale that they would find the sweets, work out it was me who put them there and subsequently befriend me over a shared delight of sugary treats. Despite the fact it didn't work I kept this up for several months.

As I grew older it became more and more apparent to me that I needed to engage more constructively at playtimes; the dilemma was that I didn't really understand how these groups of people got together, nor what they talked about when they did, or how they played together. So I used to advertise what I was going to do during the breaks and provide times and locations for my 'performances'. These were physically based; for example, I would let it be known that in such and such a location, at this specific time, I would perform 100 press ups on my fingertips. It worked a treat – people gathered around to watch and seemed impressed that I could actually do what I had said I could.

When in secondary school, however, this ploy seemed to no longer hold any appeal, and people started to disengage. I wasn't sure what to do, so did the logical thing and removed myself from breaks altogether – usually by going for a bike ride on my own.

Interactions outside of school

I used to be expected to 'go out and play', as requested by parents. There was a little play area/field nearby, which was the expected location for said 'play' so that was where I went. However, I remember watching groups of children of my age group and being terrified about having to approach them, or them approaching me. I had two brilliant (in my head) strategies for this: one, climb a tree and hide – this worked pretty well, though was a little boring and quite stressful as I had to keep a watch out in case anyone spotted me; two, pretend I was deaf and could not speak. I spent quite some time perfecting a rudimentary mime to convey my apparent lack of hearing and speaking abilities, and enthusiastically performed it as and when required. I must say I got some very strange looks; years later I put two and two together and realised that seeing as they lived on the same street as me, and many went to the same school, they must have known full well that I had no problems with my ears or mouth – but, at the time, this never occurred to me. I think this lack of awareness was actually a saving grace to a huge extent for me; if I was oblivious of the fact that I was the laughing stock, it didn't bother me! Similarly, I used to take great pride when the older 'hard' boys at school spoke to me. It was (literally) decades later that I reviewed what they were saying and came to the realisation that they were actually bullying me (or at least trying to – I must have made for a rather frustrating 'victim' for them) – at the time, though, I simply felt all warm inside that someone was making the effort to talk to me.

So – I left secondary school to go to a sixth form college. I could have stayed at the school as it had a sixth form, but I was getting rather bored at not being spoken to by my peers, and frustrated as to why this might be the case.

In the sixth form college it became clear to me that I had not magically gained the necessary skills to interact, as I had been hoping over the summer holidays. However, it turned out that this was to be quite the bonus! There was a 'common' room where attendees of the college gathered to converse with one another, and there was a table in the corner. I used to get there early, and perch upon the table, in isolation. After a few weeks of this I was introduced to a group of individuals who for one reason or another had formed a tight-fitting friendship circle, and who had decided that I was an 'interesting' person – it turns out that quite without meaning to I had been exuding an air of mystery, as I sat on my own with my odd attire (which turned out to be a good thing – seemingly I was 'cool' for not following the trend) with my look of aloof indifference upon my visage. What a bargain! So, I went from a loner to having an instant group of folk who seemed happy to call me their friend. They were a very pleasant bunch and I got on with them well; at least until I left sixth form college and never spoke to them again. I wasn't being horrible – I just didn't see the point, as our mutual commonality (college) was no longer a factor.

Ridiculous

(Please note – these are some of the things *I find ridiculous*. I am not suggesting that they actually *are* ridiculous, it may be that I am the ridiculous one for thinking them ridiculous; in which case feel free to ridicule me – I am unlikely to ever meet you, so I am not really bothered.)

Doing things just because most other people do it that way

Relationships are – pretty much by definition – personal; so why would anyone, ever, try and emulate the way that other people have relationships? It seems to me to be extraordinarily daft to assume that what works for one couple would work for another. It's hard enough trying to fit in, and pretending to be someone you're not in everyday life – I would suggest it's not the best idea for a long-term relationship!

School/college reunions

This is somewhat a bizarre concept to me. If people have fallen out of touch for several years, surely that denotes some kind of aversion to wanting to be together? Why this should change a decade or so later is beyond my comprehension.

Work friendships

I am not suggesting for one moment that friends cannot be found at work; what I do find deeply unsettling is the expectation that simply *because* one works with a group of people there is some kind of unspoken rule that one should also socialise with them. Point in case – the dreaded Christmas works get together. If anyone can explain the logic behind that they have my utmost respect.

Weddings

The amount spent on weddings – financial, emotional, time, stress – seems to me to be such a huge waste. Having to go to someone else's wedding when you really don't want to be there, and presumably the hosts don't really want you there either, but you have been invited because you are a relative or the partner of the one they really want – can't we all grow up a bit and be a bit more honest about things, which would I guess be a great relief to all concerned? By all means invite people who you really want to share the day with, but why all this angst about 'having' to invite certain people, the subsequent stress over who to sit next to whom, etc., etc.?

Getting the blame

This is specific to when relationships end. Why is it that there always has to be blame attached – usually for the person who has instigated the break-up? If someone has had the guts to realise that the relationship is not working and has the decency to end it (so long as they do it as kindly as possible), why should s/he be the default villain? It makes far more sense to appreciate the person for their honesty. I suspect that relationships are damaged badly and become messy when no one does the decent thing and end it before it gets to that stage.

Affairs

I simply do not have the cognitive capacity to understand how anyone could have an affair. To me, it's simple: either one loves one's partner, in which case such a betrayal is simply not possible; or, if one does have the wish to have an affair then presumably this is an indication that one no longer loves the partner, in which case the decent thing to do would be to end it before moving on. To me, all those arguments about how exciting an affair is, dangerous, even, shows a terrible lack of respect for the partner. If you're that desperate for thrills and spills take up bungee jumping, quad biking, swimming with sharks – don't cheat.

Having lots of friends

Friends cost – they cost time and effort, at the very least. Therefore, the more friends one has, the less time and effort one has for each of them (unless one is in the improbable position of having unlimited time and effort). Therefore, statistically, the more friends there are the lesser the potential quality there will be per friend. Thus, having a (really) small number of friends with high quality relationships is, for me at least, preferable to having lots of friends with poorer quality relationships.

Sublime

I know very few people who I have genuinely liked (the flip side being I have met very few people I have genuinely disliked; in the main I am ambivalent) – but, when I do meet someone with whom there is a connection, that connection is so deep and rich it is one of the best things in the whole world. To be understood, accepted, embraced for who you are – and to reciprocate those aspects within a relationship – is rewarding indeed. I am pretty sure I can be exceptionally difficult to be in a relationship with in many ways; but I hope and suspect that in others I am the opposite. My partner is the first person ever who has spoiled my love of being on my own, and I thank her for it. For decades I craved being on my own, quite simply because it was easy, and enjoyable. Now, though, because of my depth of feelings for her, I prefer to be in her company, and am lonely without her. I have absolute trust in her – which can be a bit of a problem as I then get stressed if she says things that are not quite true – even though I acknowledge that it doesn't matter in the great scheme of things if she is running later than she said she would, or that a planned activity is postponed, it can still be uncomfortable. However, that level of trust has had a hugely positive impact on my life; I would never have achieved the things I wanted to without her telling me I could do it. It really is as simple as that – if she tells me I can do something, instantly I believe that I can – and, as she tells me, she is always right!

I don't understand all the specifics of why we have such a good relationship, but I can have a decent guess:

- She takes what I say without prejudice – this is critical, I think. So, if she asks me my opinion – on whatever subject – she knows I won't filter my response. While to others this may come across as rather blunt, I think she genuinely appreciates the honesty and is used to my particular brand of communication.

- We certainly share a sense of humour – utterly irreverent and a far cry from politically correct, and yet absolutely without prejudice or offence to anyone else.

- She puts up with my obsessions; if I am particularly interested in something, she allows me to pursue it, even encourages it, even though I suspect it may be rather irritating to her!

- She socialises without me (mostly); this is of great relief to me. While social media is somewhat of a mystery to me I love the fact that she can socialise in a virtual sense with me reading a book next to her.

- She socialises with me (occasionally); every now and then I build myself up to be taken out for an evening with her friends. I aim to be on my best behaviour and try not to complain about it – relationships are give as well as take, after all.

- She isn't at all ashamed of me (at least, I don't think so). She went to see a film with her friends in which a character behaved in a rather odd way – I think he threw himself on the pavement to converse with a dog. Afterwards, when chatting about the film, someone mentioned how she didn't know anyone who would ever behave like that. My defiant and loyal wife quite proudly defended the fact that it was exactly the sort of thing I would do.

Some relationships I find ridiculous. Mine – is sublime.

Chapter 24

Intimate Relationships
Head or Heart?

A. Nonny Mouse

Introduction by Dean Worton

I've heard a few cases of females on the spectrum being in abusive relationships. I don't know if it's a higher instance than for predominant neurotypical (PNT) females but a range of social difficulties could be why this seems to happen all too often, and not knowing the warning signs or how to act upon receiving warning signs. I feel that people detected as being on the autistic spectrum should be offered specialist social training following diagnosis which could help to reduce or ideally avoid such issues. Being abused in any way can be very detrimental to a person's confidence, and I feel that everyone with autism needs to know that they are a deserving and worthwhile person with a lot to offer the world.

Also, when a PNT is not upfront, an interlocutor with Asperger syndrome (AS) is often unable to read between the lines, and as a result may get hurt. A message to PNT readers is don't just expect people with AS to work stuff out for themselves. It usually needs to be explicitly stated and, if you fear hurting the individual, they will be more hurt the longer you try to protect them with silence.

I was thinking round this subject for some time before I began to write and decided that, for me, it is very difficult to identify both the nature of my feelings at any given time *and* my own qualities and characteristics. This, on reflection, has had a massive bearing on my intimate relationships and their eventual outcomes. Here is my story...

As a teenager I had a few short relationships – the longest being six months and in all of these I explored the nature of intimacy with curiosity and a strange mix of head and heart. My principles at this time dictated that I did not explore in too much depth, i.e. on a wholly physical level, complete surrender. Instead I used it as a time to learn about boys, explore their motives and compare them to my own.

It is worth mentioning at this point that previously I had been subjected to sexual abuse and grooming by a family 'friend' so had rather more knowledge on a purely experiential level than many of my peers of intimacy without choice but not without a degree of physical arousal. This had informed my decision to make sure any surrender thereafter was entirely under my control. This was a valuable learning experience on a 'head' level but needed considerable counselling in adulthood to come to terms with the physical enjoyment and attention-seeking behaviour it fostered.

Aged 16 I developed an obsession with a boy in my social circle. I allowed him to dictate the terms of the 'relationship' to such a degree that many of my rules (except physical boundaries) were forgotten temporarily – surrender to heart – until eventually my head regained control and I saw there was no point in continuing. I subsequently was the subject of such an obsession and was able to have direct experience of how I must have come across earlier and again was grateful for this insight.

Quite soon after I met the man who was to become my husband and with whom I would go on to have three children. I was attracted to his simple straightforward manner and his complete honesty – so similar to my own.

The relationship progressed in a natural easy manner and we fell in love. Intimacy was unforced and he was gentle and loving throughout and as well as always enjoying it I occasionally experienced the bliss that total connection in such a way brings. Just what I needed! We both approached everything with a mixture of head and heart and were on the same page with the things we wanted from life.

However, as I mentioned earlier, I rely upon others to help me form a picture of self. I mistakenly held the view that because he loved me, he would give me a true and accurate picture. Unfortunately, after we had been married for a couple of years he intimated that I was fat and so my self-perception changed overnight and I 'gave up' and spent more and more time believing I wasn't good enough. I put on weight to match these expectations and we put our effort into bringing up our children. This became our 'job', the thing we did best and as a result our own intimate relationship suffered until at last he left, saying I had chipped away at his love. As much of the intimacy and love had already gone I once more used my head to rationalise what had happened but suffered considerably on an emotional level, having nothing in my arsenal of coping strategies to combat the situation.

The next chapter took me completely by surprise. After around a year of being on my own a long-time male friend developed into much more when he told me he wanted me to stay 'so I can look after you'. My mum had always said she had wanted someone to look after me and so this struck a chord. Up until that point I had not considered him as anything but one of my dearest friends and, after an initial beginning of physical intimacy we refrained from anything except sharing the same bed and allowing ourselves to relax into the new situation. I was able to give up my façade of coping and became more 'me' than I had ever been with a man before.

After six months we began a physically intimate connection that I had never experienced before – that connected us to source and provided energy to enable me to blossom as never before. It was during this time I received my AS diagnosis and my world and my security became complete. We were fortunate not to have to work and so were privileged to experience the freedom of shared experience untouched by others' expectations. We shared holidays, walks in the countryside and encounters with wildlife I will never forget as well as wonderful food made with love by him and meals out in great locations.

I have realised that having a deep physical and emotional connection to a partner is what inspires me to be me – to love and to care for and to hope for the same in return. Unfortunately, this person's heart belonged to another and so he could not commit to me in this way.

Again, my picture of self was put together by the things he said. Because he was not attracted to me on a physical level but said his involvement came via our long friendship, he compared me to what he had experienced with his former partner and with her qualities and with others he saw as more suitable for him. This, once again, led me to feel less than I was and again I have put on weight and 'given up' to match these expectations. I am suffering much more on a heart level this time and I am having difficulty rationalising as it affects me on so many levels.

In addition, my inability to understand my own feelings has left me open and vulnerable throughout my life to others' interpretation of my most intimate thoughts and it seems has given some the right to judge my actions and motives inaccurately. It is only after long reflection I can analyse my feelings and reach the right conclusions for me. Unfortunately this means I only realise what I am missing once it is gone, because when I am in the 'bliss zone' I am incapable of thinking with my head. I am simply being *me* and responding to my own needs by instinct, not conscious thought. If everyone was like this the world would, I think, be a happier place, for people could be who they truly are.

Perhaps us 'unfeeling' autistic folk have the edge as we think with head, heart *and* instinct and maybe as a result have much more authentic love lives. Who knows?

I suppose now I have to decide whether embarking on another relationship would be prudent given the potential for suffering. I will remain open to the possibility because of the joy that it has always brought with it. We will see...

A quick update – since writing this piece I have spent several years without any kind of intimate, physical relationship. Initially I missed the closeness that such relationships bring but later found massage to be an amazing healing tool, providing the basic need of human contact without the requirement or complications of more complex physical and emotional components.

Of course, I sometimes feel lonely for the company such close relationships provide but, on the whole, I have found the space a lack of emotional commitment affords has given me time to explore better my own needs and characteristics.

Travelling has also provided me with experience of one-to-one interactions which, I must say, I have always preferred. This gives opportunities for learning and for understanding my own value and worth without having to rely on the, often wrong, impressions others have of me.

In time, I hope to come across someone with whom I can share growing physical and emotional intimacy but am not making it my life's mission. I choose for now to work towards achieving balance between helping others and spending time with friends while sometimes enjoying my own company and space.

Everyone wants to be loved and valued for who they are, after all.

Chapter 25

Kissing the Frog

Chris Stobart

Introduction by Dean Worton

It is not uncommon for people with Asperger syndrome (AS) to prefer friends of the opposite sex. Most young people will expect their same sex friends to be similar to them in order to be 'one of the lads' or 'one of the girls', which will invariably mean being laddish if male or girly if female. AS females might be more able to mask the fact that they are different as they can get away with being quiet with predominant neurotypical (PNT) female friends more than an AS male can with PNT male friends who might tease someone who is not ladlike, doesn't like sports, doesn't drink, swear, goof around (not knowing Chris, I'm speaking generally). Many females will enjoy the company of a kind and gentle AS male who treat them as they should be treated, some would love to be in a relationship with such a guy, and thank goodness such females exist. Sadly not enough do but, as stated earlier, it's to be hoped that, as understanding of autism increases, that will change (and likewise in some cases where the genders are reversed).

A musing on Asperger syndrome and relationships

A number of things in life make me jealous. Three in particular spring to mind here though it is only the last one I will be addressing here:

- Aspies with secure jobs

- Aspies who have no problems learning to drive

- Aspies who are married.

I sometimes think that the Aspies who do best are probably the ones who brood on their condition the least. I don't know how much truth there is in that but I do remember that when I was a virile teenager and had crushes on everyone and no one when it came to the opposite sex, I felt happiest and most myself and the most able to blossom socially among those who didn't make fun of my eccentricities (I wasn't diagnosed until I was 21) or feel the need to remind me of past social gaffes. This is probably why most of my best friends at school were of the opposite sex and remain so today, even inviting me to get togethers where I am the only male of my old school present. Later years, leaving school, developing the kind of obsessive compulsive disorder (OCD) that is accompanied by religious scruples and panics, etc. brought on such a regression in me that I realised that those innocent years had gone and that the problems of my early life had never entirely gone and that something was hanging at my heels that was impacting on how I presented to others, including prospective partners, and that would probably always do so. It was around this time that I first heard of Asperger syndrome. Three years later I was sitting with my mother at a south London hospital getting diagnosed by Dr Patricia Howlin, to whom I remain indebted. Knowing I had this disorder proved to be something of a mixed blessing. On the one hand it explained so much about my early life, obsessions, fears, social difficulties, developmental and learning difficulties, behavioural gaffes that seemed to cause more offence than they merited. So many things that used to be skeletons in my closet became something I could talk openly about at social gatherings or with parents whose children had been diagnosed recently. But on the other hand it made it very hard for me to relax socially. Autistic disorders generally cause their sufferers to become obsessive about anything from their hobbies to their health and on this occasion I tended more towards the latter. I was in a very sympathetic church group at the time and I am grateful still to those friends who chose to show me tough love in telling me when my social conduct was offputting or inappropriate, e.g. dominating conversations, breaking wind audibly during sermons, or even just politely telling me I had 'an element of spamminess'. But in the end, becoming socially acceptable in my conduct became such an obsession that I have found it hard to relax totally in social situations without making fairly constant enquiry as to whether I have said something inappropriate. This lack of self-confidence cannot have helped when it came to seeking to start relationships, even in the happier and more self-confident periods of my life when (in my opinion) I was presenting better than usual. I've had a fair few unrequited loves. Some of them I was even brave enough to admit it to. But I wish I had a tenner for every time they said they only wanted to be friends with me. Most of them still are at the time of writing so I don't mind putting this here in plain sight. But from the age of 21 onwards I can't help thinking that awareness of my condition hasn't always helped and sometimes the condition hasn't helped either. I could even tell you of times when rather than doing the classic Aspie thing of missing out on signals of annoyance from people, I'm pretty sure I missed subtle signals from one or two women that they wanted to be a little bit more than friends with me. But in trying too hard to be socially appropriate, perhaps I have let other things slip.

- What would your future wife make of you being this messy?

- The only way you're going to get in a relationship is if you find another fat person.

I have had both of these things said to me. The issue of chronic unemployment also doesn't help. I have often thought that the only way I could find success in marriage would be to marry a doctor or some other member of a well-paid profession and keep house during the day – a lot easier when you've got someone else to consider and share the load with. Eligible bachelor. I hate that term. Some of us need meeting halfway to eligible. There are so many boxes one seems to have to tick to make oneself eligible. Today's culture of singles groups that teach you how to be eligible flies in the face of the motto of one of the most familiar folk tales. They would probably rewrite it like this.

> Once upon a time there was a frog. He rather fancied the princess who played in the garden where he sat on a lily pad all day long. But he was told that the only people who would ever fancy him would be other frogs unless he tried really hard. So he went to classes, bought himself a dicky bow, pretended he didn't enjoy living in slime, etc., etc., etc. until one day he hopped out of the pond and found he'd become a handsome prince. 'Thank God for that!' remarked the princess. 'I was afraid I was going to have to kiss you. You can go out with me now if you like.'

One of the best lessons I learnt in the halcyon teenage years I described earlier was that you can only be at peace with others if you're at peace with yourself. I would have done well to remember this in the years after diagnosis. As it is, while I have made some strides in social skills (occasionally taking one step back), I have gained weight as a result of much comfort eating, lost all confidence in keeping my gaff tidy apart from wiping one windowsill per day and found myself becoming more prickly and fearful. I could learn much from my 15-year-old self if we were to meet in some corridor of time.

Chapter 26

An Aspie Accord

Planet Autism[1]

Introduction by Dean Worton

This chapter is a good summary of how a large proportion of people on the autistic spectrum are likely to feel about friendships, and most likely have similar feelings about romantic relationships albeit on a much deeper more intimate and emotional level. Typically, a person with autism will have a different style of communication to someone without. Usually there will be someone out there accepting enough of such differences to become a friend (sadly not always genuine). Unfortunately, partners that are this accepting are harder to come by but I take my hat off to those wonderfully compassionate people that do turn up once in a while, and take their autistic partner as they are. After all, people with autism, although 'different' are still people, and nearly always good people often with strong moral values.

What does friendship mean to me? It means a feeling of comfort with someone – not feeling like you have to make conversation being in their presence; no pressures – the knowledge that if you don't contact them for a while, they

---

1 Planet Autism is the online 'entity' of the author of this chapter.

won't hold it against you; being able to converse at length – and if I monologue a little they will find it interesting and listen. I rarely click with people, I keep my distance and make little effort with meeting people. Why? I have Asperger's. I don't know how to start up conversation without feeling very awkward and because I can't make small talk without great difficulty, this is a hindrance to the 'normal' way of getting started. But that suits me fine because so few people are on my wavelength anyway, I'd rather meet them in a fortuitous way.

Sometimes, we find we are thrust into situations where we have to communicate with people, such as through work. I recall starting one friendship purely because I have a strong sense of justice, and when another colleague was victimising a new girl, I deliberately went out of my way to counteract that and help her. I hate someone being made the underdog and that friendship lasted a while. Although I was naïve to the fact that she was jealous and was gossiping about me behind my back. Things floundered when I played a too convincing practical joke and she fell for it, her mother was furious with me. There was no harm done, other than some disappointment on her part, but things were never quite the same. Was that me being unempathic? Did I not know when I had taken a joke too far?

Other friends have been a lot older than me and sort of adopted me, which I suspect is because I came across as sensible. Being older, they have been mature and wiser than younger peers and that has suited me. I have never had a group of friends. The few friends I have had over time, those who have had slightly Aspie qualities have been the most enduring. My best friend from school was shy and introverted and we also laugh at the same things, it's across the miles these days though, as she emigrated.

No friendship is perfect, the same as any type of relationship, people can let you down or behave in ways you don't understand. What I have found, is that friendships with others with Asperger's are more straightforward. Neurotypical people, or 'NTs', are much more complicated and it's harder work maintaining the friendship, they seem to expect something out of the friendship and I don't always know what. People with Asperger's say what they mean and mean what they say, the chances of lies are a lot less and it's harder to offend one another. There is no pressure or bitterness about reciprocity in the friendship from what I can gather. Aspies understand one another in a way that NTs can't understand Aspies, and vice versa. I don't mind listening to another Aspie monologue, so long as it's not about train timetables or Pythagoras's theorem – although if it were the workings of vacuum cleaners that might be different ☺! When I converse, I don't like gossip, but if someone has a problem, I will try to find practical solutions for them. Some NTs find this akin to comforting them and being a good listener, but an Aspie will likely appreciate the workings of your mind and the fact that you have given them a solution. This is great for bonding. NTs seem to like gossip, small talk and using social media to connect. I use social media for one reason, a community autism page, not for chatting and heaven forbid the 'friending' of random people! I see no benefit to clocking up friend numbers on Facebook. NTs wear this with pride. I would rather have one or two decent friends I clicked with than 25 acquaintances I couldn't trust.

I think talking about emotions (for instance to therapists) doesn't work for many on the spectrum. We don't want to (and often can't) ramble endlessly about feelings, we want practical solutions. So if an Aspie is upset about a problem and an NT friend hugged them and said 'everything will be OK' that wouldn't be inordinately helpful to us. So a friend who was very touchy-feely in that way might make an Aspie feel uncomfortable and irritated.

People with Asperger's can fall victim to 'mate crime', so it's important that we have friends that don't take advantage of our relative naïveté and other Aspies are not going to do that. Social games are complex; I'm usually oblivious to them. I can tell if someone is angry, or overtly sarcastic, or upset, etc. but I cannot tell if someone is being nice in a fake way and I don't get that they might have ulterior motives for befriending me. In my personal experience, with another Aspie, I won't have to worry about anything like that, the games are not there full stop.

Both my daughters are on the spectrum too, and both of them are having socialising problems at school. My heart sinks for them, as I know through their lives they will find out the hard way what people can be like. They are struggling to know if people like them, receiving nasty comments from other girls who clearly recognise they are different. Neither has a best friend. So I endeavour to educate them about people as much as I can, but I am already at a disadvantage to do so, because I still struggle to understand people myself. There can be a silver lining to those clouds though, because at least we can speak about our experiences together and know we are not alone in our difficulties. I am still disappointed when I find out people have lied to me and deceived me. If someone is nice to me, I think they mean it. This has let me down so many times, but is often par for the course if you are on the spectrum. I don't want my daughters to be hurt like that and it would be nice if they could find some Aspie friends to click with, to reduce their difficulties.

So, I don't have any issue if my friends are NT, but they will always be a certain type of NT – as 'Aspie-like' as possible – and I wouldn't have it any other way.